The Redundancy Survivor's Field Guide

Use your redundancy to re-direct your career

The
Redundancy
Survivor's
Field Guide

Graham Till

how to books

First published in 2003 by
How To Books Ltd, 3 Newtec Place
Magdalen Road, Oxford OX4 1RE, United Kingdom.
Tel: (01865) 793806. Fax: (01865) 248780.
email: info@howtobooks.co.uk
http://www.howtobooks.co.uk

British Library Cataloguing in Publication Data
A catalogue record for this book is available from the British Library

Cover design by Baseline Arts Ltd. Oxford
Produced for How To Books by Deer Park Productions
Typeset by Pantek Arts Ltd, Maidstone, Kent
Printed and bound by Bell & Bain Ltd, Glasgow

Contents

Chapter 1
Surviving redundancy

THE PURPOSE OF THIS BOOK IS TO PRESENT A SYSTEM WHICH WILL TURN THE TRAUMA OF REDUNDANCY INTO A PLATFORM FOR HITHERTO UNDREAMED SUCCESS.

So you are facing redundancy! Like many thousands of other people each year, you have been thrust into this situation and probably didn't want to be. Are you haunted by the prospect of reorganising your work and life? Are you struggling to cope with unwelcome emotions of fear and anger? Or are you already planning your next positive career/life move?

You are now faced with a series of wonderful opportunities dauntingly disguised as a terrible and unwanted situation. This chapter introduces two key concepts:

- your innate power to achieve incredible success;

- a unique job-getting system to harness and focus your personal power.

Although primarily for job-getters, this book is not just about getting another job. The real purpose is to mobilise your personal power to turn the trauma of redundancy into a platform for hitherto undreamed of success. It is more than a survival manual – it offers a method which will bring success that far exceeds mere survival. Many will decide to seek another job, although not necessarily in the same industry or even in the same line of work. The key word is 'decide'!

The first secret is that decisions make winners. This book offers you a winning system which produces winners but you must *decide* to change things yourself. The aim is to help you identify and achieve the things you desire most in work and life. The Globeskills PSP system, described later in this chapter, is an immensely powerful job-getting method. However, this book is also a key to the treasure chest of work/life success. That is a big claim, but the power is awaiting your decision to take conscious control of it.

So, how can you unleash your personal power? You can release the force within you simply by deciding to claim it! This is the major step that you must take *now*. Remember, whatever might have happened to you in the past and whoever might have been responsible, your only point of personal power is *now*. The actual decisions that change lives only take fleeting seconds. Moreover, if you don't claim your personal power and make the decisions yourself, then something or someone will make your decisions for you. You will be at the mercy of your environment. So, take conscious control and decide to make strong decisions to succeed, right now.

Decide to change. Make decisions about what lifestyle you want for yourself, what job you are going to do, and decide that you *are* going to achieve it. There can be no backtracking. Commit yourself to a life of success and reward. Decide who you want to be.

Your destiny is altered in such moments. The moment you make these decisions, you must also decide that your commitment to them is non-negotiable. Even when things go wrong, even when the path ahead seems dark and gloomy, stick with your decisions. Once your decisions are made, live your life by them. You will ultimately achieve your goals. This is the key to success.

It is a very simple formula. Yet few people actually take control of their lives by making such committed decisions. We all have to make important decisions through-out each day, yet most people never actually commit themselves to life goals. They are like corks on the tide, bobbing along with the current, swirling with the whirlpools, washing up on the sand and floating off again, surrendering control to the surrounding environment. This is the one major difference between winners and losers. Regardless of other conditions, such as privilege, luck, wealth and education, success invariably comes to the people who make a massive decision to succeed. Talent alone cannot succeed – there are many talented but unsuccessful people. Unrewarded genius is so common that it has become a cliché. The world is littered with highly educated failures. Many offspring of wealthy parents have ended up as derelicts, despite their privileged start. Only persistence and focus is omnipotent. Guaranteed success is only achieved by a committed decision followed by deter-minedly focused action.

You can achieve huge success whatever your personal history or circumstances. Don't make excuses in anticipation of failure. Right now, you need big decisions, not excuses. Only decisions can alter your destiny, not the conditions that currently inhibit you. In fact, you will find strength and valuable, unique experience in those conditions.

Decision-making is the trigger for massive and unstoppable personal power within each of us. You merely have to make truly committed decisions to initiate action for success. The next secret is to focus the resulting incredible force with the intensity of a laser beam. To do that it is necessary to identify and define your targets.

RIDING THE SIGMOID CURVE

The sigmoid curve is an ancient concept that sums up the story and timeline of any part of life, and even of life itself (see Figure 1.1).

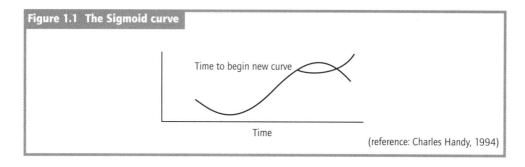

Figure 1.1 The Sigmoid curve

Time to begin new curve

Time

(reference: Charles Handy, 1994)

Everything has a natural lifecycle and the sigmoid curve illustrates it as a skewed, flattened S shape. You can apply this concept to any kind of lifecycle. The curve plots the rise and fall of lives, products, political movements, love and personal relationships, empires, dynasties, companies and so on. The theory is very simple: when something new is started we initially make slow progress by trial and error, then we eventually learn and find effective methods and grow rapidly until we reach the maximum possible level before beginning to fall away.

For the purpose here, the sigmoid curve illustrates the rise and fall of any stage in your career. This can apply equally well to a specific job or to a phase in your working life. So, there are two clear requirements:

▇ to ride the wave that you are currently on, knowing that it will peak and eventually fall away;

▇ to judge the right time to create or catch the next wave to ensure your continued growth and progress.

It is obviously preferable to start a new cycle *before* the first one falters. As far as your job is concerned, the fact that you have been made redundant clearly shows that it is already too late for that to happen. However, that doesn't mean that it is too late to seriously consider the current wave that is your career direction and the type of work that you do. The trick of using the sigmoid curve is to calculate the likely timescale and then determine where you are now on the curve. This is not always easy, of course. The time measurement of each lifecycle differs. Modern technology and our hectic lifestyles have combined to produce some significant, relatively new factors:

▇ the compression of time;

▇ an accelerated wave frequency;

▇ the constant paradox of change.

Job and career lifecycles used to take decades to unfold. In fact, very often a person could stay in the same job for the whole of his or her working life without much evidence of any change at all during that time. Now, though, timescales are dramatically shortened and the resulting acceleration of pace affects us all. So career curves have shrunk and rarely stretch for a lifetime. Unlike our predecessors, most of us can now expect to have to change our jobs and careers a number of times in our working lives if we are to survive and progress.

Thereby lies a paradox: we are often still locked into a traditional way of viewing jobs and careers when change moved more slowly, even imperceptibly. This inertia – the tendency to use false milestones and measurements – means that often we only see the downturn after it has occurred. You are almost never positioned on the curve where you think you are, and are usually much farther along it than you care to acknowledge.

THE PARADOX OF CHANGE

The best point at which to start a new cycle is obviously before the top of the curve. This, of course, is just the time when everything seems to be going really well on your current wave. It can seem almost irresponsible to change. This is the conflict between the visible comfort and dependability of the old (or current) career and an unfelt need for something new and different in the immediate future. We tend to choose inertia because we seem to be fine the way we are, often despite nagging doubts. Consider how this description fits with your experience in your last job and it will doubtless be a very close match.

It is natural that you are only really motivated to change direction when your current cycle is literally over the hill. Unfortunately, problems are more difficult to deal with at a time when things are escalating downhill at increasing speed and when your energy, resources and time are ebbing away too. It is much better to start the new wave when you are still approaching the summit of the old one, when you have the time, energy and resources associated with comfort and success.

So, even as you prepare your next step, bear in mind that you need to prepare for the next wave too. And later, even as you enjoy the peak experience of the next move, you will know there will eventually be a need to begin another move and run it concurrently. Know that you will need to judge timescales accurately and redirect resources and energy as you see the next core career fading and accelerating downhill. It's like building a new house while continuing to live in the old one rather than waiting for it to fall down. It needs insight, courage and determination to build the future while at the same time maintaining and extending the present.

Bearing that in mind, take a few minutes right now to do the following exercise and begin to identify your goals. This is a first 'run-through' and you should revisit the exercise when you have had more time to absorb the concepts of this book. If you have the help of a trusted friend or career coach, then you should go through this process with that person on a number of occasions until you are happy with the result. When it is right for you, then you will know it.

Goals are dreams which you feel in your heart can be achieved.

Exercise 1

1. Take five minutes to brainstorm a list of goals that you would like to achieve. Allow your imagination to run free and think the unthinkable. Write a list of all the lovely things that you would like to achieve, anything that comes into your head, as you imagine luxury and utter success. Goals are dreams, and you should dream big! There's no need to go into detail – just note keywords so that you can remember your idea.

2. Goals need to be viable. They need to be physically possible for you. Note that the word 'realistic' was not used. For too many people, realism equates to defeatism and continuing surrender to the harshness of life. Go through your list, one by one, and decide if you have the resources to achieve each goal. Mark those goals where you are short of some key factor.

3. Look at your list again, and go through those goals where you know that you need more resources. For each of these, make an objective decision as to whether it might be possible to gain the missing factors. Score out only those goals where you deem it definitely, utterly, totally impossible to add the relevant resources. Remember 'difficult' does not mean 'impossible'.

4. Now, go over your list and decide a preliminary timeline for each remaining goal. How long will you give yourself to achieve it? Do not be afraid to use long lead times: two years, three years, five years, ten years... Remember, that your future career is now likely to be a series of linked short- or medium-term curves, each one starting before the last has peaked. Some of these will be quite similar kinds of work and style while others may be totally different.

5. Now choose *just one* of the goals that you *will* achieve in the *first year*. This is the immediate one! Its status might change at a later stage in your journey, of course. Other goals could overtake it in priority as you take advantage of circumstance, but it will remain a committed goal.

6. Now write two paragraphs that describe why you have chosen this goal. State which relevant resources you have, and how you will achieve any resources that you do not currently possess, what steps you will take. Why is this a good idea? What are the obstacles? Who might be able to help you? Describe the first steps that you will take.

7. Now write two more paragraphs that describe the results of your success in this goal. Give the date and state what have you gained, the great rewards it has brought you, and how you feel about it, your personal fulfilment, what it has meant for family and friends, your lifestyle, and so on.

That is a first trial of the method. You will need to repeat the exercise a number of times as you develop your ideas in the coming weeks. That is how you will eventually set your most highly valued and viable goals. Once you have defined your targets, this book reveals several techniques for reinforcing your indomitable drive to achieve your goals. The next requirement, however, is a map which shows the practical way to achieve them. You need to create an action plan to make your dreams come true.

A WINNING JOB-GETTING SYSTEM

Once you have identified your goals you then need to devise a strategy and appropriate tactics to achieve them. Plan your work and work to your plan. Identify interim goals – the next steps – and then systematically set out to achieve them. When you make your map, remember that the map is not a picture of the terrain. What seems relevant from one dimension or in theory might not necessarily be true in practicality. Be ready to change your planned route to get to your goal. This, of course, is not the same as abandoning a decision. Your strategy to succeed remains constant, but your tactics might change.

What steps are you taking to acquire the necessary skills and experience to enable you to obtain your desires? The highly effective redundancy survival system used in this book was developed by studying thousands of redundancy survivors and identifying how they succeeded. The question asked was this: '*Is success merely a chance and random result or did the winners share common ingredients which enabled their achievements?*'

A study of people in many large-scale redundancy situations was conducted over a number of years. The aim was to determine what things, if any, the successful people did so well to set them apart from their unsuccessful colleagues.

This method, then, derives directly from a study of success and excellence in the field of job-getting and life balance. It will show you how to emulate winners in surviving redundancy – those people who turned it to their own advantage.

THE WINNERS

Inevitably, there are plenty of examples of people who apparently succeeded through sheer good luck and with little or no planning. Knowing the right person or merely being in the right place at the right time continues to be the best way of getting a job. Indeed, almost everyone can tell you of a friend who chanced to land a job in this way. However, the study showed that in those circumstances it is rarely the *right* job. Anyway, appearances can be misleading: successful candidates often create their own 'luck' through methodical networking and by deliberately *putting* themselves in the best position at the appropriate time. As a successful person once said to people who considered him fortunate in the chances that came his way, 'It's funny, the harder I work the luckier I get.'

The study revealed that most consistently successful people are remarkably focused and organised in their career/life methods. They search out advantageous circumstances and give themselves every chance to profit from them. They take the trouble to list and make contact with all of the people who might be able to help in achieving their goals.

There were four major discoveries:

1. Most of the successful applicants treated each career goal as a separate project. This meant giving separate and special consideration to producing a targeted CV and a self-marketing letter tailored to the target, then following through with a structured interview plan. In the case of self-employment they had a detailed business plan, carefully researched, with staged interim goals.

2. Whether by instinct or planning, the majority of winners narrowed their job-getting tactics to four or five main selling points – their *Prime Selling Points* – strongly emphasising their ability to ideally satisfy the main criteria of each job.

3. While concentrating on the four or five key points, consistently successful job-getters also included general qualities to present a well-rounded and attractive package.

4. The central strategy was invariably implemented with a methodical self-marketing system. They systematically ensured that they saw all relevant job advertisements, embarked on a campaign of speculative approaches to employers, and used employment agencies. They invariably kept good records, and efficiently planned and maintained their job-searching schedules.

By making decisions, setting their goals, organising their job-getting activities and targeting employment applications with the precision of a laser beam, these winners made it easy for recruiters to select them for interview and, later, to award them the job. Many winners demonstrated that they were able to amend and deploy the same techniques with other employers, competing for different jobs with equal success.

It appears that the fact that they were working to their own agenda and well-prepared gave them the added sparkle of confidence which counts for so much when meeting potential employers.

THE LOSERS

The winners' stories contrasted starkly with hard-luck tales related by many unsuccessful candidates. Many of those who failed at the last hurdle had been convinced that they had done really well: they often felt that they had 'had a good interview'.

The reason for this was that they had no agenda of their own. They had just turned up as passive victims to be interrogated; their only goal had been to answer every question without making any awful mistakes. They had no 'sales plan', and no strategy to concentrate on pre-decided selling points. Losers rarely targeted the *core competencies* of the job or enterprise. They wasted precious interview and meeting time on irrelevant side issues when they should have been ruthlessly demonstrating their ability to satisfy the central, vital requirements of the job.

Unfocused and unprepared candidates were usually poor judges of how they had performed at an interview. This is understandable. Professional recruiters are trained to be friendly and encouraging to interviewees; this often leads less discerning applicants to feel that they have performed especially well, and their disappointment is all the more acute when the letter of rejection arrives.

THE GLOBESKILLS PSP SYSTEM

The common success factor is to be found in satisfying the main and central points in the minds of the people you are trying to influence. If you are seeking a job, then you must convince the recruiter that you have the necessary key competencies. If you are promoting a business, you need to convince potential backers and sponsors that your idea is viable in the main, key points. In either case, it also needs an efficient method to implement an effective self-marketing strategy.

These observations are crystallised into the Globeskills PSP – *Prime Selling Points* – system which enables anyone in a redundancy situation to achieve success. The result is an integrated suite of techniques which concentrates upon taking aim at specific career opportunities, rather than an unplanned blanket-coverage job search (which is usually driven by the next job advertisement you happen to see).

The *Prime Selling Points* (PSP) system is a highly focused job-getting system which has proved itself in the pressurised environment of many mass redundancy projects, helping literally thousands of people at all levels to quickly resume their careers. PSP involves looking at a job and analysing the key skills, experience and qualities that are essential for that job. These are labelled *Key Competencies Required*. They are then matched by the candidate's own tailored *Prime Selling Points*.

The PSP system involves the balancing of two central elements:

■ *The job*: the main skills and attributes at the core of the job in question:
  - *Key Competencies Required*

■ *the candidate*: the package of skills, experience and qualities offered by the candidate for the specific job:
  - *Prime Selling Points*

While the *Key Competencies Required* will vary from job to job, there are a number of 'constants' or general competencies which apply to all of them. Every CV and job application in some way takes account of the following:

- communications

- planning and organising

- goal orientation

- personal integrity

- teamworking

- problem-solving.

Some of these general competencies will carry more weight than others for particular jobs. However, nothing is left to chance and you must cover them all. There are exercises in this book to help you develop a comprehensive analysis of your own competencies. This will enable you to demonstrate that you satisfy the selection criteria under each of these headings.

The central concept of specially targeted Prime Selling Points backed by an impressive array of general competencies is supported by an effective administrative, organisational and self-marketing system, also detailed in this book.

No presumption is made regarding the job level of readers. The Globeskills system is a complete, integrated and holistic job-getting method which works with any kind of job at any level. Whether a scientist, truck driver, company director or cleaner, the same methods will be effective. What you need are determination, persistence and hard work. Getting a new job is a job of work in itself but the rewards are well worth the effort.

Figure 1.2 describes in broad terms the various stages of the Globeskills system. It is simple and straightforward. Job searching is simultaneously carried out on at least three separate levels:

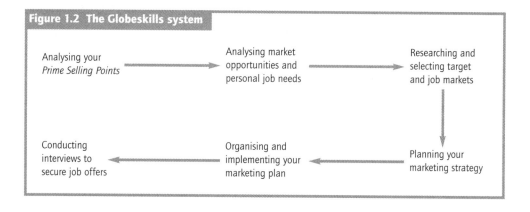

Figure 1.2 The Globeskills system

Analysing your *Prime Selling Points* → Analysing market opportunities and personal job needs → Researching and selecting target and job markets

Conducting interviews to secure job offers ← Organising and implementing your marketing plan ← Planning your marketing strategy

- advertised job markets;

- hidden job markets;

- recruitment agencies/headhunters.

The system fits together as a coherent whole. By using it you will:

- realistically identify and verify your stock of skills and experience;

- consider your preferences and priorities for your career development;

- prepare your job-getting plan;

- organise an efficient job search record-keeping system;

- examine and evaluate your general competencies, e.g. goal orientation, team-work, etc.;

- identify your preferred career goals and appropriate job markets, and select your *Prime Selling Points* for each market;

- produce effective CVs;

- thoroughly trawl each job market for both advertised and unadvertised potentially suitable job vacancies;

- analyse job vacancy advertisements;

- fill in application forms in an effective way;

- network to find potentially suitable vacancies and opportunities;

- plan and implement a speculative letter campaign;

- use the telephone effectively in your job search;

- use a personal computer in your job search campaign;

- analyse the requirements of each job, and identify its *Key Competencies Required*;

- from your own stock of skills choose your *Prime Selling Points* for the job in question;

- prepare your targeted job application – CV and accompanying documentation;

- prepare, practise and perform winning interview techniques geared specifically to the target job and your *Prime Selling Points*.

Try it now!

Exercise 2

As a first step, you need to establish some basic information about yourself. Try this exercise, giving particular attention to Question 8:

1. What is the title of your current/last job?

2. Briefly describe the duties of your last job.

3. What job do you want to do in the future?

4. What is your biggest achievement?

5. When did you last attend a job interview?

6. What aspect worries you most about the process of getting another job?

7. If you were recruiting a person to fill your present/most recent job, what would be the four most important skills or attributes in the ideal candidate?

8. How do the answers to these questions relate to the main goal that you identified in Exercise 1?

It is quite likely that your new main goal might not sit easily with your other answers. This is a process of self-discovery and conflicting answers promote self-awareness rather than invalidate your aims.

SUMMARY

This opening chapter has introduced two key concepts:

■ the power of taking control of your life by making strong decisions to succeed;

■ the Globeskills PSP system.

It has concentrated upon the need to first identify your clearly defined, viable goals, and then to follow through with the planned and highly focused action embodied in the PSP system. The combination is irresistible. The theme of the book is already established: make sure that you commit yourself to your decisions. Remember, clarity gives power, so make your goals clear and unambiguous.

When you have established your clear goals, use the PSP system to produce the results that you really want for your life. Treat every unsuccessful move as good feedback for your personal map-making. Continually test your actions. If it isn't working, then keep changing until you find something that does work for you.

Four steps to success:

1. Clearly decide what you want.

2. Take massive focused action to make it happen.

3. Notice what is working and what is not.

4. If it isn't working, change it for something else and keep trying until it does work.

Anyone can succeed if they apply these steps and keep on applying them.

Chapter 2

Key competencies

HAVING ALREADY IDENTIFIED THE TWO MAIN STRATEGIC STRANDS OF THIS BOOK, THIS CHAPTER LOOKS AT THE KEY UNDERPINNING OF THE GLOBESKILLS PSP SYSTEM: *KEY COMPETENCIES.*

WHAT ARE *KEY COMPETENCIES*?

Key Competencies are central to the whole system of *Prime Selling Points*, so it is necessary to define what is meant by the term. The definitions we are using here refer to what is known as the behaviourist approach. They refer to the personal characteristics that produce a superior performance and enable some individuals to be better than others in any job and work environment. The International Labour Organisation gives a number of definitions of *Key Competencies*:

'*…understood as the knowledge, attitudes, skills, capabilities, values, conducts and personal attributes in general that are (coincidentally) related more directly with a successful performance of people in their job, functions and responsibilities'.*

'*key personal characteristics … define what the person is and are reflected in all they do. They are particular characteristics that go from deep and central aspects of individuals to relatively easily observable and modifiable aspects'.*

'*set of abilities, skills, pieces of knowledge and attitudes in terms of observable conducts…'*

'*personal characteristics that differentiate between the adequate and the excellent performance, in a specific position, in an organisation or culture. They are certain ways of doing things; they are those behaviours and abilities that people demonstrate when conducting a task with excellence'.*

'*observable and measurable knowledge, abilities and skills as well as characteristics associated with an excellent performance…'*

'*set of abilities, skills, pieces of knowledge, attitudes and values, whose application at work translates in a superior performance, which contributes to the achievement of key objectives of the business'.*

Key Competencies are vitally important to both recruiters and job-getters. The recruiters usually begin by identifying the competencies they seek and then evaluate each candidate against each competency. In this way, they conduct a systematic search for the best available candidate and assess his or her suitability for the job. Even untrained recruiters subconsciously follow the same type of reasoning.

It should, incidentally, be remembered that some recruiters seek to match a list of competencies that shows the person is suited to the organisation, and not just to the specific position. They consciously seek people who have an abundance of competencies required for different jobs and environments characteristic of their organisation. It is therefore possible to be awarded a job in preference to another candidate who, on the face of it, has more specific claims.

Any individual possesses an array of competencies and, it follows, is deficient in others. Many would claim that some characteristics can only be changed in minor ways, although they acknowledge that others can be acquired and developed. They would claim that things such as attitudes, values, conducts and reactions, personal interaction and so on can hardly be modified. However, the PSP system is based on the premise that most competencies can be acquired and nurtured.

It is clear that your package of characteristics *must* coincide with the model the enterprise requires or you don't get the job. So, in each instance, you need to assemble and present the characteristics and attributes that the occasion demands. That knowledge informs the whole basis of the Globeskills PSP system. The aim is to ensure that you offer and focus tightly upon the very competencies that the recruiters are seeking. This makes it easy for them to award the job to you.

Selection methods are becoming increasingly rigorous and sophisticated, often including tests and/or exercises. It is necessary to be very thorough when preparing your approach. It is not enough to merely claim that you have the required competencies; you must make sure that you actually possess them. So it is important to first of all analyse and evaluate your *Key Competencies*. It may then be necessary, using the methods discussed later in this book, to consciously acquire and cultivate certain desired characteristics or attributes that you lack.

This chapter concludes with the first general competency exercise. You will find five further exercises in Appendix A. The purpose is to examine each of the selected general competencies. They are designed as a series of questions, much like those you can expect to be asked at an interview. Working through these exercises as part of the PSP system will provide suitable evidence that you possess these general competencies in greater or lesser measure. This is an important part of your preparation and it will be valuable when defining your goals, writing your CV and informing your decisions.

Choose your own way of approaching this. What works for you? You may want to do all of these exercises immediately. Or you may want to do three of them and then return later to complete the other three. Alternatively, read the book and then return to the exercises. You decide but, whichever method you choose, please make a decision now to complete these exercises and the others in this book to build your conscious and subconscious store of self-knowledge. Also, you will probably be surprised how often these or very similar questions are asked in actual interview situations, so it is helpful to develop easy familiarity with them.

This chapter supplies a commentary for the first exercise to illustrate the general method of answering the questions. Subsequently, however, you will get more from the exercises by doing your own analysis, looking at why the interviewer is asking each question and what he or she is trying to assess by your answers.

Each exercise concludes with a score sheet. The scores will indicate your current strengths, and also any areas of potential weakness that you need to address.

GENERAL COMPETENCY EXERCISE 1:

COMMUNICATIONS

The first general competency exercise is also probably the most important. A good set of communication skills is the basic, vital tool in your job search. It is not just a matter of selling your skills and potential to a prospective employer. An interviewer will assess evidence of your ability to communicate effectively with others.

The ability to communicate effectively is a fundamental skill required by all human beings. We instinctively begin to learn from an early age: an infant soon finds out how to communicate wants and needs in a way that is likely to get the desired response. Effective communication is more than a matter of words: tone, facial expression, enthusiasm, appearance and, particularly important, listening are all vital elements.

Like most other skills in life, some people develop more effective communication skills than others. Natural ability and talent have something to do with this, but environment and differing needs are probably a greater factor. For example, salespeople need to be particularly effective communicators. They learn the art and continually polish their abilities on a daily basis, often through unconscious trial and error: an approach which proves successful is used again and improved upon while less effective ploys are instinctively abandoned. On the other hand, a manual worker probably feels only a limited need for a high level of communication skill; that situation can quickly change if the person is promoted or is required to act as a group spokesperson.

Indeed, the situation changes dramatically if a person is job-hunting. In other words, when job-hunting, you need to learn to communicate in a way which is likely to obtain the results you desire.

Think of the bad impression given by a poor communicator typified by these two extremes:

- the timid person who has a limited vocabulary and lacks fluency – this person cannot easily relate to others and displays low self-esteem;

or

- the arrogant and overbearing sort of person who does not listen to others, giving the impression of making up his or her own mind before considering other views – someone who rambles on at length and tells rather than discusses or persuades.

YOUR IMAGE

You are a person who enjoys talking. You enjoy contact with others and are able to get to know new people quickly. You can build a good rapport with them. You look for opportunities to listen and, more importantly, are able to learn by listening to others. You are persuasive and can communicate successfully, in writing or orally, in one-to-one situations and to groups. And you express yourself well when interviewed.

This describes the person you are seeking to portray. If you read the description again, you will probably see that, to a greater or lesser extent, you *are* that kind of person. The main task is to demonstrate it, particularly during an interview. Don't forget that dress and personal appearance are also elements of good communications.

Take an A4 pad and work through the following sets of linked questions. Save your answer sheets for future reference.

Set 1

(a) Give an example of a time when you were especially successful at communicating something either orally or in writing.

(b) How successful were you on that occasion and why?

(c) How did you assess your efforts?

If you analyse your answer you will probably find that it satisfies only a part of the criteria set by the interviewer. Does your example illustrate successful dealings with a group? Or a one-to-one situation? Does it describe oral communications? Or written? The chances are that you will have chosen a rather narrow example which covers only certain elements of the criteria you need to address.

With a little thought, you can probably find a situation which involved all aspects of the definition, for example a particular project when it was necessary to deal first with individuals face to face to discuss ideas before producing a detailed proposal that communicated plans and ideas in writing. This may then have been followed by a group presentation centred upon your report. During the ensuing group discussions, by listening to the contributions of others, you might have slightly amended the plan, but been able to persuade others of the merits of your proposals.

Such an example gives positive evidence of both oral and written communications, in one-to-one and group contexts. It also demonstrates:

- good presentation skills;

- an ability to listen to the views of others;

- an ability to synthesise ideas;

- an ability to persuade people to accept your point of view.

You will probably be able to come up with something similar from your own experience. If you cannot think of any examples which cover all of the points, then provide one example which satisfies most of them.

Set 2

(a) Can you describe a situation when it was necessary for you to listen carefully to what someone was telling you?

(b) Why was it important that you listened on that occasion?

(c) What information did you get by listening carefully that you might not otherwise have got?

Great talkers are rarely great listeners. You should choose an example where you were able to pick up on relatively understated objections or concerns. Indeed, the concerns may have been unspoken and expressed by verbal opposition to other less important factors. Show that you actively seek opportunities and contrive appropriate circumstances to listen in order to find out the other person's point of view.

Give evidence that you are able to learn from others by listening. Demonstrate that you can gather relevant information in this way. As a bonus, show that you can use the discovered knowledge effectively – addressing hitherto unidentified conflicts, for example.

Set 3

(a) Think of a time when you needed to establish a good rapport with a person who was important to you in a work context. Who was this person and why was he or she important to you?

(b) What skills were required, and which did you lack?

(c) How did you overcome your own lack of any particular skills to build a good relationship with this person?

Tricky! Questions of this type will frequently arise in interviews, so it is best to practise dealing with them. Choose an example that involves a person who was important to the aspirations of the organisation rather than to your own ambitions or purposes, e.g. a customer. Incorporate evidence of your ability to behave appropriately and build a sound, ongoing relationship. Also show that you can identify the needs, likes and dislikes of other people. Provide evidence of forethought and planning, and demonstrate your ability to identify and address other people's doubts.

Set 4

(a) Describe an occasion when you had to communicate something to people of different corporate levels.

(b) What were the main factors you had to consider?

(c) How did you accommodate the factors to communicate effectively?

This is to assess your flexibility and adaptability. Your example should demonstrate preparation and a willingness to learn. Choose with care. Demonstrate your commitment to equal opportunities without appearing completely obsessed by it. Show that you can easily relate to people from all walks of life, simultaneously if need be. Difficulties may include language, cultural differences, class perceptions, differing aspirations and priorities of different groups. Show that you can analyse and accommodate the issues and devise an effective method of communication.

Set 5

(a) Describe a situation where you had to persuade someone to change his or her opinion, or get them to do something that they did not want to do.

(b) What did you do to achieve this?

(c) What level of success do you think you achieved, and why do you think it?

It is probably best to choose a situation where a reasonable person held sincere views which were in conflict with the aims of the organisation. Resist the temptation to describe a bloody conflict with a pig-headed boss: that just casts doubts on your ability to build and maintain a good relationship, particularly with superiors. You are seeking to show that you are able to build rapport – say it in so many words, if possible. Give evidence of planning and listening skills. Importantly, say what feed-back you obtained to indicate how successful you had been. Note the emphasis on evidence.

SUMMARY OF EVIDENCE – COMMUNICATIONS

Spend a few moments reviewing your answer sheets. Then make an assessment of your answers against the statements in the left-hand column of the chart on p. 20. Give each a score of between 0 and 6, where 0 = fails to meet any part of the state-ment and 6 = meets all aspects of the statement. Address any area of weakness by returning to the relevant set of questions and try to produce a more effective answer.

COMMUNICATIONS
SUMMARY OF EVIDENCE

Assess your own answers in this summary, giving yourself a score from 0 to 6.

Fails to meet any part of the statement   *Meets all aspects*

Evidence	0 No evidence	1	2	3	4	5	6
Ability to communicate concisely and effectively							
Enjoy talking and dealing with others							
Persuasive skills							
Able to build effective relationships							
Good listening skills							
Able to overcome the resistance of others							
Able to plan and implement effective group communications							

Aggregate score: _____

For each of your past **4** jobs, choose a good example that demonstrates your communication skills (use your previous answers if desired):

1 _____

2 _____

3 _____

4 _____

Chapter 3
Dealing with emotions

REDUNDANCY IS A TIME OF GREAT STRESS AND EMOTIONAL TURMOIL FOR YOU. THIS CHAPTER PROVIDES YOU WITH THE TOOLS TO DEAL WITH IT.

'It is not the strongest of the species that survives, nor the most intelligent – but the most responsive to change.'

Charles Darwin

If you are like most people who have been made redundant then you will have taken a lot of emotional baggage on board. Research and experience show that redundancy affects everyone emotionally to a greater or lesser degree. It seems to be inevitable and it may even be a necessary stage that is akin to grieving, because it is a significant change in your life. Recognise that, and know that everyone goes through it.

It is typical to experience a welter of different and contradictory emotions. Some of these feelings seem impossible to reconcile with other reactions which are felt with equal intensity. One moment things will seem incredibly clear and the next you cannot see the forest for the trees. Fear of the future often alternates or coexists with excitement. And no wonder – you are engaged in a major life change. When it comes to inducing stress, it is widely accepted that redundancy ranks with the death of a loved one. In fact, there are many similarities between losing a job and bereavement. The respective models that describe the typical patterns of emotions are very similar. This similarity isn't surprising. When you lose your job, you are dealing with the death of a very significant and important part of your life. Traumatic change has been thrust upon you and it is healthy and normal to experience a train of mixed emotions. The pattern will be broadly the same for everyone although each person will behave differently, of course: the timing and duration of each phase can vary tremendously and different people respond to their emotions in different ways.

The model in Figure 3.1 shows a typical and common behavioural pattern derived from studies of a large sample of people who were dealing with redundancy. The human brain is remarkably adaptable and geared to survival. It usually finds a way to cope if left to its own devices. On the other hand, we can help it considerably with our own actions if we have a rudimentary understanding of how the brain works.

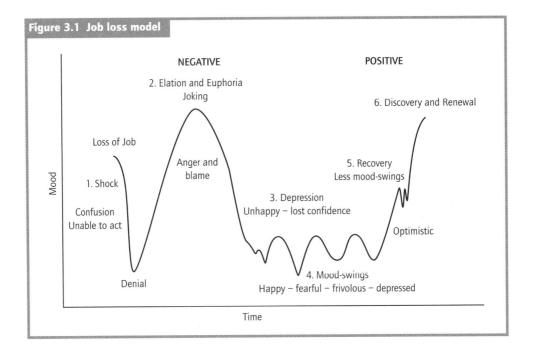

Figure 3.1 Job loss model

A BRAIN OF TWO HALVES

Research in the past 50 years has shown that the left brain and right brain each perform various specific functions. Some of these functions cannot be carried out by the other half.

Left (logical)

Our left brain does the job of conscious thought. It is the logical half of the partnership and responsible for reasoning, critical analysis and planning. Importantly, it is also the engine for thinking in words, which is necessary for us to codify and articulate our awareness. That awareness refers to both internal feelings and external events. Throughout every waking minute, each of us silently 'talks to ourself' to analyse and rationalise things that are happening and, hopefully, explain them in a way that we can understand. We are verbal creatures and we communicate with others and ourselves by using words.

Right (emotional)

The right brain looks after emotions and feelings. This is the unconscious mind involved in visualising and imagining things or situations. It doesn't reason. Neither does it deal in time or logic: it can 'feel' an emotional hurt that was sustained years ago just as intensely as if it had happened yesterday. That is illogical, you might say. This demonstrates *the* important point: when the emotional right comes into conflict with the reasoning left, emotions will always defeat logic. Emotions take over, even though you try to keep logical control.

This is not to say that the two halves aren't working together. Indeed, the two hemispheres act as a partnership and communicate through a system of connecting nerve fibres. One role of the left brain is to try to understand the right brain's feelings and put them into words. There is considerable overlap and we effortlessly switch between the two from moment to moment for the most mundane tasks.

For the most part, the central purpose of your combined brain is survival. Any significant situation such as redundancy is complex and vast. To give it meaning, you reduce things to simple terms. In other words, you make a 'mind map' for survival, leaving out some things and including others, depending on what you decide is important. It all depends on the filters you use to sift the information.

On the other hand, it seems that the emotional right brain can work on its own, independent of its partner. The filters it is using are not selected logically (which does not mean they are inappropriate). Clearly, the pattern shown in Figure 3.1 shows the emotion-based right brain in action. A purpose of this chapter is to show you how to persuade your right brain to maximise useful emotions and quickly release and replace those that are unhelpful. The aim is to enable you to access the unconscious part of your brain and use it to move smoothly through the phases of the job loss model.

The important thing is to deal with emotions in a positive way. Some redundancy counsellors advise taking a few minutes to consider the emotional aspects of redundancy. The theory is that by recognising and articulating your feelings, you are able to deal with them in a rational and logical way.

However, this book advocates spending at least two days devoted entirely to yourself and your emotional and physical well-being, and including some gentle self-hypnosis. The term can alarm people but it merely refers to a natural method of deliberately choosing to invoke and use normal mental processes that we all experience each and every day of our lives. The general aim of self-hypnosis is to achieve an altered state of conscious awareness and that is precisely what you are seeking in your goal to reinvent yourself.

TAKE TIME OUT FOR A REDUNDANCY DETOX

Choose a couple of days when you have plenty of time to give yourself a redundancy detox without interruptions from other people. A whole weekend might be difficult for some people because it's a time when family might be around the house more than usual. On the other hand, many newly redundant people can find time alone during the week. Anyway, the important thing is to avoid distractions where possible.

First decide when you are going to set aside a few days for this important new beginning to prepare and clean your personal space.

DECLUTTERING AND CLEANING

This might take you a week or more, working as and when you feel it is right for you. This is essential preparation for the detox, however. It is more than just just tidying up your home and ensuring that necessary chores are all done (although this is important of itself, otherwise nagging guilt or irritation could spoil your relaxation during the detox.)

Your aim is to consciously 'declutter' your space. Start by removing from your life those things that are no longer relevant, necessary or appropriate. As you work through your home and belongings, look at each item in turn and assess whether you want or need it around you any more. Be particularly ruthless with stuff that is connected with the job that you have just left. Keep only those things that are important to you and your future. Otherwise, get rid of it! Dump it, send it to charity shops, give it to friends… anything, so long as it goes. If you are jettisoning some previously important item, then don't look back as you walk away.

If possible, make a bonfire in the garden. There is a lot of satisfaction and healing in ritually burning papers and objects that once seemed so important in your old job. Say 'thank you but goodbye' as each piece disappears in smoke. On a deeper level, be aware that decluttering your physical space is connected with decluttering your mind: reassessing your ideas and values, removing outdated beliefs and limitations, sweeping away obstacles, clearing away the cobwebs and making your mind-space a generally brighter and nicer place to be.

TOOLS FOR THE DETOX

While all this is going on, remember that you are spending this time preparing to pamper yourself. Assemble a few necessary things:

- stationery – get a good notebook, preferably hardback, and some smaller notepads;
- candles of various scents and colours;
- essential oils, moisturising lotions or creams, colognes;
- skin exfoliation products, cleansers, creams and moisturisers (men choose from the various excellent ranges of male products that are available – but do it!);
- decaffeinated tea and/or coffee or fruit tea sachets;
- clean face flannel or small towel;
- hand mirror and large mirror;
- books – including this one – and magazines;
- audio relaxation tape (there are several available);
- cassette player;

◼ for men, nostril and ear hair clippers;

◼ food – make sure you do your shopping beforehand so that you don't have to go out during the detox period. Get plenty of mineral water. Include nuts and seeds in your shopping list. Make sure you get lots and lots of fruit, including strawberries, peaches, papya, mangos – and not just for eating but for a luxurious and exotic cleansing treatment. And, if this is your thing, treat yourself to a nice bottle of wine (this is not the typical, spartan detox!).

If it is winter, turn the heating up a notch or two. Make sure that you have plenty of hot water for some nice, long baths, with soft clean towels and a good selection of bath oils and other favourite toiletries.

IMAGE AUDIT

Before you start your detox, take a good, long look at yourself in a mirror. Review your general appearance and personal hygiene routines. This session can literally bring you face to face with some things that you may prefer not to deal with at this time, when you may already feel vulnerable. However, remember that the grand objective is to change your life! You should treat the image audit in a disassociated way, as if objectively studying another person. Be candid and realistic in your assessment and not unduly harsh. Remember also that this is not about being Superman or Superwoman, or striving for the body beautiful. If that were the case, where would most of us be? On the contrary, this session is about making the most of your own potential with good hygiene and presentation and some realistic decisions and actions.

Bearing that in mind, take some time now to look at yourself in the mirror and assess your image to see how you can improve it. Remember to check from the sides and the back too (the reason for the small hand mirror). Get your notebook and make any relevant notes as you consider your appearance and grooming.

Hair

First, do you usually wash your hair every day with a frequent-use shampoo? If not, then you should make it a new rule. This is particularly necessary for people with naturally greasy hair but it also benefits dry hair, removing the daily grime. Those people who suffer from dandruff should use a medicated shampoo and keep a small clothes brush handy to dust off the shoulders, especially before important meetings or interviews. It seems that some people can never fully resolve a persistent dandruff problem, and for these people it is recommended that they wear medium grey jackets and suits.

Does the cut suit the shape of your face and complement your figure and size? Is the style of your hair compatible with your ambitions and the type of job that you would like to do? Long hair on men, for example, too often looks scruffy and unkempt in a working environment. If you are in the slightest doubt make a decision now to change your hairdresser and go to the best that you can reasonably afford, asking for advice. Nor should men shun the *expert* use of colour or other treatments, particularly if they feel, rightly or wrongly, that an aging appearance is a detrimental factor.

Eyebrows, nostrils and ears

Make sure that your eyebrows are trimmed. Most women tend to be very attentive to this feature, but men often need encouragement to tidy their eyebrows and make sure that they are clearly and separately defined. Men, especially those beyond mid-life, should take this time to use the specially recommended electric clippers to trim their eyebrows. They should also remove unwanted hair from ears and nostrils, which can be very offputting to others.

Men's facial hair

Image consultants who advise politicians know that men with moustaches and beards are less readily accepted by most people than men who are clean shaven. On the other hand, a weak male chin can be an even bigger hindrance; in that case, the recommendation is to create your own strong shape by growing a beard.

That said, studies reveal a deep prejudice by many people against men with facial hair. Apparently it is all to do with subliminal primordial messages, about having something to hide and being darkly menacing. Whether this is true or not, the fact is that clean shaven men usually have a better chance of getting a job. Make your own decisions on the matter now.

Hands and fingers

Are you content that your hands will be a good advertisement for you in one-to-one or small-group meetings? When you shake hands firmly (a must, incidentally) will the other person wince at the rough skin? Be honest with yourself and decide to take any necessary action.

The strange thing about other people's hands is that we only tend to notice rough and badly manicured ones and yet a lot of people fail to notice their own failings in this respect. The appearance of your hands is very important, because they are on display for such a lot of the time. You don't have to have perfect, shapely 'soap advertisement' hands, of course, but you should make sure that they are manicured and well-maintained. It might be well worth a visit to a professional manicurist, although many men would baulk at this. As a general rule, soak your hands in warm, soapy water for a few minutes each day, and clear any dirt from under your nails. Buy a good hand cream and use it daily to keep your hands soft and smooth. Each week, spend some time clipping, filing and polishing your nails. Always keep a supply of medium- and fine-grade emery boards and buy a nail-buffer to promote a nice, healthy sheen. Cuticle cream is also a good investment.

Personal hygiene, deodorants and fragrances

Different scents appeal to different people, as evidenced by the multi-million pound fragrance and cosmetics industry. However, nobody likes the whiff of stale body odour, and we all sweat, especially when under pressure or nervous.

So everyone needs at least one bath or shower each day. And everyone should use a deodorant of a suitable strength or type according to how profusely you sweat and the sensitivity of your skin. There is little point in bathing and then putting on clothing impregnated with sweat, of course. Make a strict rule that every day you wear clean underclothes and clean shirts or blouses too.

Scents, aftershaves and colognes should be carefully chosen, erring towards the subtle and understated. Make sure the fragrance complements your persona rather than overwhelming it with cheap, cloying perfume. Also, it should be compatible with your own specific body chemistry because the same fragrance can change its effect when worn by different people. Aim for a clean, light and fresh scent and, if uncertain, do not use it at all. Remember that a good quality deodorant soap will give your body a fresh and usually very subtle scent, and this is often enough for most occasions. On the other hand, if you do find a fragrance that particularly suits you and fulfils all the criteria, it can be wonderful for your image.

Shoes

Do your shoes do you justice? Men should remember that thick rubber soles might be comfortable but they give a very downmarket image. A woman's appearance can be totally ruined by scuffed heels and unpolished uppers. So aim for neat styles that bespeak discreet style and attention to detail. Polish your shoes daily, preferably as soon as you take them off, when the warm leather will more easily absorb the polish. And try to have enough pairs of shoes to allow a good rotation, giving time for rest and increasing longevity.

Working clothes

Look into your wardrobe and appraise the range of clothes that you wear for work. Are they suitable for the new image that you want to portray? To project a successful and professional image – remember that is your aim – your clothes must be the best that you can afford, both in terms of style and quality. Money is obviously a factor for many people. If you have to make the best of the clothes you already have, make sure that they are clean, pressed and in good condition.

IMAGE ASSESSMENT

Now complete the image assessment questionnaire on p. 28.

YOUR IMAGE ASSESSMENT

Rate yourself for each factor by ticking the appropriate box	Poor	Average	Above average	Excellent
Handshake: is it firm and friendly, without being overly strong?				
Eye contact: during conversations, do you look people in the eye frequently but for short periods of time, avoiding a fixed stare?				
How do you assess your daily standard of grooming and appearance (personal hygiene, hair, face, hands, teeth, etc.)?				
Is your posture and deportment as good as it can be (taking account of any physical disabilities or limitations)?				
Are the clothes that you currently wear for work suitable to project the successful image that you are seeking?				
Taking account of accent and dialect, how do you rate the quality of your voice in terms of compatibility with your desired image?				
Is the vocabulary that you tend to use habitually devoid of slang and swear words?				
Social skills: are you comfortable when dealing with people at all corporate levels?				

Score your image assessment ratings as follows:

Excellent:	5 points
Above average:	3 points
Average:	1 point
Poor:	0 points

If you scored more than 24 points

Congratulations! You are an image-conscious and aware person who aims to project an appropriate appearance. Don't rest on your laurels, but continue to strive for the best presentation that you can achieve in various situations.

If you scored between 16 and 24 points

This probably means that you are very good in some aspects, quite good in others, but only average in a few key areas of your image. You just need to work on the weaker points that you have identified.

If you scored between 8 and 16 points

Average! This isn't necessarily a wholly bad thing but, by definition, you are on a par with most of the rest of the herd and won't impress recruiters with your presentation. You need to work on your overall image and push it beyond the average mark at the very least.

If you scored below 8 points

You currently have a very poor, almost unmarketable image. You are not a hopeless case by any means. In fact, this is one of the easiest and most significant things that you can change to make a huge difference to your future. Make a decision to systematically address each area of image and appearance and start to make changes immediately.

SUMMARY OF THE IMAGE AUDIT

Are you making the best of your personal appearance? Can you improve the impression that you give to the outside world by improving the way you dress and physically present yourself? Maybe a new hairstyle or hair colour might be called for. If you decide that this is the case, then it's best to get it done before you undertake the detox. Perhaps your wardrobe and style might need updating? If so, as a part of your preparation, try to buy at least one significant item of clothing that 'signposts' the change of style.

BATHING IN CANDLE LIGHT

On the evening before the selected detox day, complete your final preparations. Place the cassette player complete with audio relaxation tape beside your bed. Also put a small notepad and pen on your bedside table and others at strategic places about the house: ideas come at the most unexpected times and places and you don't want to lose them. Now, lock the doors and unplug the telephone. Pour a tumbler of mineral water and take yourself off to the bathroom. The purpose is not merely to wash yourself, but to symbolically cleanse your whole being and wash away your troubles and stress, draining them down the plug hole.

Warm a towel and place it in your bathroom. Draw a deep, pleasantly warm bath, adding your preferred bath oils or foam. While the bath is filling, slowly drink a full tumbler of mineral water. Now place three unlit candles in the bathroom, making sure that they are in safe positions that can be seen from the bath; if the candles are fragrant (pine is good for this purpose), then so much the better. Name each candle as you set it in place: Past, Present and Future.

Light each candle, saying its name as you do so. Get into the bath and for the next five minutes simply lie back and luxuriate in the scented water. Simply concentrate on the feeling of warmth that permeates and relaxes your muscles and soothes your mind. Try to clear other thoughts by noting and dismissing them.

When you are suitably relaxed, transfer your concentration to the candle you have named 'Past'. As you do so, think about the things that have happened in your own past. As you transfer each thought to the flame, consider how you feel about it. Don't dwell on your thoughts or try to be too deep. It's best to accept without question the thoughts that come into your head. After two or three minutes, still concentrating on the candle, try to identify the emotions you have been experiencing. Think of a single sentence that describes how you feel and say it out loud.

Now move on to the candle that represents your present. Repeat the process, not trying to be too intense, but concentrating on the burning candle until you have arrived at a single sentence that sums up your feelings about the present. Again, say it out loud because the spoken word always reinforces inner thoughts.

Finally, concentrate on the third candle: Future. As you watch the flickering flame, decide what you want to happen in the future, what you really want for yourself. First thoughts are often the most genuine and truthful. Summarise them it into a single sentence and say it out loud!

Now, try to remember each sentence – soggy notepads have no place in this exercise. Repeat the sentences for Past, Present and Future, silently comparing each with the others. Then consider the immediate goal that you identified in Exercise 1.

That's it! Almost without effort, you have identified emotional factors that are key to you. There is no need to do anything about it. Your two brains will organise things between them. Instead, just lie back and soak for a while. As you lie there, visualise the stress leaving your body and dissolving in the water. When you are ready, get out and dry yourself.

As you blow out each candle, repeat the sentence you have attached to it. Then pull out the bath plug and watch your stress swirl and glug away. Be good to your body and lavish it with fragrances, powders, moisturisers, whatever.

Then go straight to your bed with its crisp, clean linen, and take this book with you for some important bedtime reading. Most importantly, immediately before turning off the light, write down your three thoughts from the candle bathing session – Past, Present and Future – on the notepad beside the bed. They are the things that shape you, and they will inform the rest of your job-search and redundancy survival activities. You can be assured that your brain will be working away at these thoughts even while you sleep.

Chapter 4
Embracing change

CHANGE IS CONSTANTLY OCCURRING IN OUR LIVES, TURNING EVENTS FOR BETTER OR WORSE. THIS CHAPTER SHOWS YOU HOW TO EQUIP YOURSELF TO BENEFIT FROM CHANGE.

'If you keep on doing what you always did, then you will always get what you always got.'

Change is neither good nor bad in itself – it is just change. It is not a gradual or smooth process and it moves in sudden fits and starts. In the world of work in the twenty-first century, after a long and relatively stable period for much of the twentieth century, we are certainly facing some quite dramatic changes.

Your most important career decision is the one that not only equips you to deal with change but, crucially, enables you to benefit from it. This is the single greatest commitment to your future that you can make. A major feature of redundancy is that it is one kind of cross-roads in your life and only you can choose which direction you take. There are very few opportunities like this in your life. Paradoxically, while you may not have chosen the redundancy situation, it has delivered the opportunity for you now to *choose* your future direction.

Every new journey begins not with a footstep but with an inner thought and decision. You should follow it through to a logical conclusion and continually add new skills to your own package of selling points.

THE EASIEST PERSON TO CHANGE IS *YOU*

You cannot easily change anyone else, nor can you markedly change the world around you. But you can change your own attitudes and methods, and this does not mean settling for second-best at work. Financial considerations will always bring their own counsel but they do not have to debar you from a job that you really enjoy doing. Anyway, many enjoyable jobs are often well-paid, too.

The first choice you face is simple enough. You can either…

▨ make a positive plan to profit from opportunities which the new working patterns offer, improving your career prospects, job satisfaction, status, lifestyle and income…

or …

▨ hope for the best and continue in much the same way as before.

Everyone faces these choices. Scientists, unskilled workers, computer analysts, skilled manual workers, office administrators… we are all in this same, changing world of work. Surprisingly, perhaps because of inertia and a lack of self-confidence, the majority of people at all levels choose to do nothing. They surrender their destiny to the whims of fate.

So, whatever your current work situation, from now on you should always be planning when and how to create or catch the next wave.

SHORT- AND MEDIUM-TERM PLANS

There are two aspects to any effective career development programme: the short and the medium term. In the short term, harsh reality might sometimes dictate that you need a job, and you do not have the time or the means to undertake prior training. This does not mean that you should take just any job. Your main rule should be that, from now on, any job you do should fit into your general scheme for the future.

In the medium term you should plan to develop your own relevant skills package to match your aspirations for the future. Start today. Take advantage of any relevant training or further education that you can get. Do not be deterred by the demands this makes on your free time, because it often opens up a new and interesting social world. Get your priorities right. Consider Table 4.1.

Table 4.1   Which factors will reduce or improve your chances of achieving the future that is right for you?

- *Your willingness to adapt your skills to a new environment.*
- *Your willingness to undergo retraining or further study.*
- *Your own values* – wages, success, ambition, security, working hours... (remember that they change!).
- *Your ability to shake off bitterness and anger from the past.*
- *Your interests and hobbies* – what are they? you will need to list some on your CV. they can often be converted into job opportunities.
- *Your likes and dislikes* – isolation, noise, crowds, dealing with people, heights, temperature, fumes and smells, repetitive work, responsibility, working in a team, creativity, making things, doing paperwork...
- *Your ability to listen to advice and know what makes sense.*
- *The way others see you* – learn how to present a good image to the world. Read this book and follow our advice.
- *Your friends and peers* – do not be just one of the herd. Decide what you want and aim to get it.
- *The kind of jobs open to you* – if your choices are limited and the available work does not appeal to you, improve yourself and train for a different future.
- *Your mobility* – you will not help your chances by confining your job search to a three-mile radius of your home! How far are you prepared to travel each day? The more mobile you are then the better your chances of getting a suitable job. If necessary and practicable, move home!
- *The help you are given* – do not get utterly reliant on others. Without effort and commitment on your own part no amount of help will get you a job.

Can you do anything to change the factors which may reduce your chances?

SKILLS AND ASPIRATIONS AUDIT

What kind of new skills should you aim for? That will depend upon the kind of person you are. Take some time to look at your skills, priorities and preferences as outlined below. You can then begin to rationally consider how they might translate into an effective career plan and take steps to fill any gaps in the skills relevant to your ambitions.

SELF-ASSESSMENT EXERCISES –

STRENGTHS AND WEAKNESSES

The object of this series of exercises is to develop some ideas about your own work-related skills and analyse whether your strengths are with people, things, technology or ideas. Which of these general categories do you feel most comfortable with? Which skill areas do you excel in? Which have brought the best achievements? As a very broad start, begin by just quickly assessing each of these categories, and mark whether you regard it more of a strength or a weakness.

GENERAL SELF-ASSESSMENT EXERCISE 1

Tick whether more a strength or a weakness.

Skill area	Strength	Weakness
Working with people		
Working with things		
Working with technology (IT and data)		
Working with ideas		

This is a very sweeping generalisation, of course. In reality, you will have a wide spectrum of both strengths and weaknesses in each category, but it is an overview of your own comfort zoning. To examine the concept further, let us now proceed to develops the analysis in more detail.

How do you relate to people?

THE COMMUNICATOR

Written – you can...

▨ express ideas in writing and produce concise and accurate documents

Verbal – you can...

▨ relate to people from a wide variety of backgrounds and talk easily to others
▨ persuade people
▨ be a good listener
▨ explain clearly and logically
▨ discuss intelligently
▨ speak in public
▨ negotiate.

	Strengths	Weaknesses
1.		
2.		
3.		
4.		
5.		
6.		
7.		
8.		
9.		
10.		

How suited are you to working with machinery, equipment and materials?

THE TECHNICIAN

You can...

- make and repair things
- solve practical problems
- find and rectify mechanical faults.

Do you...

- prefer to work with your hands?

	Strengths	Weaknesses
1.		
2.		
3.		
4.		
5.		
6.		
7.		
8.		
9.		
10.		

How creative are you?

Do you lean towards the artistic and creative skill sets, using intuition and ideas? Can you organise yourself? Are you innovative and able to come up with new ways of doing things?

THE CREATIVE WORKER

Are you...

- inventive?
- artistic?
- innovative?

Can you...

- find effective ways to present and communicate thoughts, ideas and feelings?

	Strengths	Weaknesses
1.		
2.		
3.		
4.		
5.		
6.		
7.		
8.		
9.		
10.		

Data and numbers

THE MATHEMATICIAN

Can you...

- understand, use and manipulate figures?
- apply figures to everday situations?
- keep accounts and ledgers?
- create and use spreadsheets?
- correlate and interrogate data?

	Strengths	Weaknesses
1.		
2.		
3.		
4.		
5.		
6.		
7.		
8.		
9.		
10.		

GENERAL SELF-ASSESSMENT EXERCISE 2

Write a general profile of yourself _____

_____

What are your greatest strengths? _____

_____

What are your weaknesses? _____

_____

Describe the role in your most recent job _____

_____

Choose the 4 or 5 *Key Competencies* demanded in that role _____

_____

What did you like most about the job? _____

_____

What did you dislike about the job? _____

_____

Choose your **4** strongest *Key Competencies* (consider if they are the same ones as those used in your most recent job).

1 _____

2 _____

3 _____

4 _____

GENERAL SELF-ASSESSMENT EXERCISE 3

Using information from previous self-assessment exercises and taking into account the skills areas that you have highlighted as your strong points, write a short statement about what you are offering an employer.

_____

_____

_____

_____

_____

_____

_____

_____

_____

_____

_____

_____

_____

_____

Make the statement short and to the point (maybe 100 words), and demonstrate the qualities, skills and experience that an employer will find attractive.

SELF-ASSESSMENT EXERCISES –

OPPORTUNITIES AND THREATS

For all sorts of reasons, it isn't always easy to locate your place in today's job markets. Finding the *right* job needs a systematic and carefully thought-out strategy. It may also mean that you need to change your approach, and even change your way of thinking about work and career issues.

Setting out on a new and different career is an exciting opportunity to make changes for the better. However, all opportunities carry some degree of risk. Taking calculated risks are what life is all about but it is important to assess the extent of each risk and whether you really want to expose yourself to it.

Look at the list below and consider which of the options might offer you a real possibility of positive change.

	Yes	No
New and different career direction		
Same field with career advancement		
Same field at similar level		
Self-employment including consultancy		
Buying a business or franchise		
Emigration		
Portfolio of different jobs		

Now separately consider each of the above categories. 'Brainstorm' a list of the opportunities and corresponding threats in each category, sticking to the major aspects (detail should come later). The list of potential concerns might include finance, key competencies and your available transferable skills, training needs, markets, significant family or social issues, likes and dislikes, life aims, work/life balance, and so on.

Select the major possibilities and analyse the opportunities and threats, using one of the grids provided below.

New and different career direction

What are the alternatives? In the first grid, take a general look at the possibilities. Consider your skills set and competencies. Will they need bolstering with retraining or qualifications? Are there any funds or grants available for training? What is the entry salary likely to be, compared to your needs and aspirations? Will it mean relocating your home?

	Opportunities	Threats
1.		
2.		
3.		
4.		
5.		
6.		
7.		
8.		
9.		
10.		

Does anything immediately stick out as a strong possibility? Have you the necessary skills? Is it possible to make a seamless transition without retraining or taking a lower position? Look at all aspects of the option and ask yourself if it is viable.

	Opportunities	Threats
1.		
2.		
3.		
4.		
5.		
6.		
7.		
8.		
9.		
10.		

Same field with career advancement

Is this a realistic option? If so, what will you have to do differently to achieve advancement, and what are the associated risks? Are you bound by any contractual restrictions? Consider which companies are likely to have a need for your skills. Will it mean relocating your home? Consider, also, the best position that you are likely to get immediately, and how high you are likely to climb in the long term.

	Opportunities	Threats
1.		
2.		
3.		
4.		
5.		
6.		
7.		
8.		
9.		
10.		

Same field with similar level and role

Is this an attractive option? Will you be happy continuing on your present path? Is it likely to be a buoyant employment market in the future? Consider pay and benefits.

	Opportunities	Threats
1.		
2.		
3.		
4.		
5.		
6.		
7.		
8.		
9.		
10.		

Self-employment including consultancy

In the first grid, take a general look at the possibility. Consider your skills set and competencies. Will they need bolstering with retraining or qualifications? Are there any grants available? What about tax and accounting? Can you make enough money compared to your needs and aspirations? Are you cut out for the insecurity? Will you enjoy the freedom?

	Opportunities	Threats
1.		
2.		
3.		
4.		
5.		
6.		
7.		
8.		
9.		
10.		

Does anything immediately stick out as a strong possibility? Have you the necessary skills, finance and equipment? Ask yourself if it is a viable proposition viable.

	Opportunities	Threats
1.		
2.		
3.		
4.		
5.		
6.		
7.		
8.		
9.		
10.		

Carry out similar Opportunities/Threats exercise for any other categories that you added, drawing up your own grid.

This is known as a SWOT analysis (Strengths, Weaknesses, Opportunities, Threats). It can be used to methodically consider anything that needs deep consideration.

To conclude the exercise, write a short statement of no more than 100 words, summarising your feelings, characteristics and abilities matched with the most viable and attractive options for your future.

THE CHANGING WORLD OF WORK

The organisation, structures and patterns of work began changing rapidly in the 1970s. This is certainly accelerating and, in many ways, is rather bemusing. Some features are easily seen:

- Large-scale, low-tech manufacturing is relocating to Third World and former Eastern bloc countries, taking advantage of lower production costs.
- Multinational companies constantly seek ways to enhance profits by moving resources and facilities around the globe.
- Service industries are becoming increasingly dominant in the UK

There is not one single job market, then. There are several markets, each responding to different stimuli; when some are buoyant others are depressed. The challenge is to respond to the many changes and turn the situation to your own advantage, moving from dying industrial sectors and trades to more modern, virile job markets.

CHOOSING YOUR JOB MARKETS

Keeping in mind your immediate goal and the subsidiary possibilities determined in the previous exercises, you should now list up to *five* job markets that may offer you the kind of job that you want. To qualify this, you should indicate the type of position that you may be able obtain in each selected market. Your list might include only one or two sectors, of course.

It is probable that local, national and international conditions will differ, even in the same industry. You should therefore list these as separate job markets. For example, a job-search in the engineering industry confined to Surrey is likely to differ from a national job-search for the same kind of position. This applies both to your personal requirements and to the job itself.

Your list will probably change in the light of experience and information gathered during your job-search. Some ideas may be eliminated, while others might be suggested and added to your marketing plans:

TARGET JOB MARKETS

	Job market	Target position(s)	Geographical area

Now, in the left-hand column, rank these markets in order of importance, taking into account your personal preference and estimated likelihood of success. The intention is to attack all of your target markets separately but simultaneously. Where necessary for best use of resources, however, you need to give priority to your best bets.

Chapter 5
Differing perspectives

MANY PEOPLE GEAR THEIR THOUGHTS SOLELY TO THEIR OWN POINT OF VIEW. THIS IS NATURAL ENOUGH, BUT HERE WE FIRST CONSIDER THE SUBJECT FROM THE RECRUITERS' PERSPECTIVE.

In the previous chapter you have taken an objective look at yourself from your own perspective. The purpose was to consider your possibilities and aspirations and to identify key aims. If it was as simple as that, the book would end here and you would simply claim your prized career. However, there is another major factor to contend with: the recruiters and employers.

So, keeping firmly in mind the thoughts that have begun to form as a result of your self-exploration, it is now time to consider these other important players in the arena. This is a central concept of the Globeskills job-getting system. Many people gear their thoughts solely to their own point of view. This is natural enough but here we first consider the subject from the recruiters' perspective.

THE RECRUITER'S VIEWPOINT

You can look at any experience or event in at least three different ways:

1. From your own point of view.

2. From the point of view of the other party who is directly involved.

3. From the point of view of an impartial, dispassionate person who observes the event but is not directly involved.

In the first case, you simply ask, 'How does this affect me?' The second involves placing yourself in the other person's position, asking 'What is this person seeking, and how does it look to him or her?' Thirdly, you ask, 'How would this appear to an independent witness?'

Most people use each of the three points of view to a greater or lesser extent. The most successful people in any field usually have the ability to move freely between them and this is a skill that is worth developing.

When it comes to job-searching, most people gear their thoughts to their own point of view – their hopes and needs and chances of success. This is natural enough. But in this chapter we first consider the subject from the recruiter's perspective.

LEARNING ABOUT RECRUITERS

How do recruiters work? What do they want? What are their likes and dislikes? Knowing the answers to these and other basic questions is essential if your job-search is to be anything other than hit and miss. An unskilled fisherman who merely baits a hook and dangles it into the water could be lucky and land a big fish. The aim here, however, is to remove the chance element by using a methodical system.

THE 6 Ps
Preparation, Presentation and Practice Produces Perfect Performance

---

WHO ARE THE RECRUITERS?

The term recruiter refers to any person who has the job of selecting and hiring people for employment. Recruiters come in various guises. They may be:

- human resources managers or personnel managers;
- line managers (e.g. production supervisors, chief quality engineers);
- technical staff;
- managers or owners of small companies;
- lay-people (e.g. charity trustees, city councillors or school governors);
- recruitment consultants;
- industrial psychologists…

This list is not exhaustive. In some situations – perhaps the majority – there will be a combination of professional personnel advisers and technical managers at some stage in the recruitment process.

Personnel managers and HR specialists

These are usually the people who will sift through the applications and prepare a shortlist. They are partly on your side already and will interview you first. Remember their own specialist agenda is to implement company HR policies and this will often take precedence over any technical claims you may have. They may not be empowered to offer the job but they can certainly prevent you from getting it.

Line managers

These people have a different agenda to that of the HR staff. They are accountable for the department and want a person who will supply direct benefits to the departmental team. Providing you do not fall foul of company policies, it is they who will usually say 'yes' or 'no' to your appointment.

Line managers are often poor interviewers. This is not their specialist skill. Their questions may only invite a single word response but you should take the initiative and expand on your answers to demonstrate your *Prime Selling Points* for that job.

Recruitment and management consultants

Outsourcing is now prevalent in business and the use of external consultants is an increasing trend in UK industry. They will rarely know the technical details of the job or even the industry, but they will be looking for specific competencies. These people usually perform initial shortlisting interviews. They are anxious to show their worth to the employer and present a good shortlist, so strong candidates find themselves 'pushing on open doors'. Be confident and assured, and concentrate on your communication skills, goal orientation and so on.

Industrial psychologists

Often psychologists administer and deliver a psychometric test. It is a good idea when faced with this sort of interview to avoid negatives about personal problems, career dissatisfaction, etc. Smile and be calm and confident. And don't be intimidated by the notion of being interviewed by a psychologist – they are as 'normal' as the rest of us.

> It is your responsibility to convey all the information about yourself, your achievements and other attributes, regardless of the skills of the interviewer.

How recruiters work

It is a mistake for the job-getter to assume that every recruiter is skilled in selection techniques. Indeed, there are as many 'bad' recruiters as 'good' ones. So, when making a job application, how can you tell what kind of person the recruiter will be? In the absence of any other intelligence (a friend who has already been through the selection process with the same company, for example) you simply cannot know in advance. You must prepare a job application strategy that will cover as many eventualities as possible, both regarding the many different systems of recruiting and different types of interviewers.

The serious job-getter must take a middle road and use a method that applies equally to both trained and novice recruiters. Think, then, rather in terms of a 'tool-set' that all managers use, consciously or otherwise, when selecting people for employment.

This 'catch-all' tool-set is organised here into a logical system, although unskilled recruiters will rarely use such a methodical approach. Equally, a trained interviewer may use one of several different systems. However, the same basic principles will underlie their thinking whether they know it or not, and the Globeskills system encompasses them all. Our system is based upon identifying and satisfying the core key requirements of any given job. To remind you again, these are identified as the *Key Competencies Required* and the means of demonstrating that you satisfy the recruiter's needs are termed your *Prime Selling Points*.

THE RECRUITER'S WISH LIST

Put simply, the recruiter's 'wish list' details the things that he or she needs from the person who will fill the job. This list might be written in a logical and systematic manner (it certainly will if the recruiter is a trained HR professional). In a small business it may be a mental checklist carried in the manager's head. Nevertheless, there will be a list. With all types of manager, the aim in any selection process is to determine which candidate best satisfies the needs on their 'wish list' and to judge if the best candidate satisfies those needs well enough to justify his or her employment. To do this recruiters study 'the form' of each candidate and ask questions that are designed to winkle out information that shows the person's ability under each separate item on the wish list. Whether trained or otherwise, consciously or not, every recruiter works in this way to a greater or lesser degree.

Recruiters are doing a job just like the rest of us, and they are judged on the success or otherwise of their selections. Their decisions can be crucial to the company's success or failure.

Never feel self-conscious about setting out to impress by calculatedly concentrating on the points you think are on the manager's wish list, even if you think that your actions are transparently obvious. On the contrary, the recruiter will love it because he or she wants to achieve the required results with the least hassle and difficulty. A recruiter will naturally lean towards the candidate who makes the job of selection easiest and the most troublefree.

> Recruiters lives in the hope that the next person to enter their office is the ideal candidate.

LEARNING HOW RECRUITERS WORK

All recruiters have their own methods. You will therefore need to be flexible when applying the PSP formula to your own real-life situation. To get an overview, we first look at the issues surrounding a typical job vacancy. Names and places have been changed but the situation is real enough. The process will be the same for virtually any type of vacancy at any level.

The job vacancy arises

In a typical situation, when a need for an additional staff member is identified by the line manager within a large organisation, he or she will contact the human resources or personnel department.

Line managers will frequently have different agendas from their HR/personnel counterparts: anyone responsible for running an efficient production or service department will usually, above everything else, be seeking a reliable and suitable person for that section, whereas the HR specialist will probably be more interested in candidates who fit wider company recruitment criteria and policies. You can do little about this (and, usually, you cannot even discover the relative power relationships between the different parties in a company), but at least you can be aware of potential dangers.

For example, the human resources or personnel people will probably receive and sift all applications first. In all likelihood they will know only an outline of the technical details attached to the job, but they will be methodical, working to lists and established criteria, and be very aware of general selection factors in employee relations. Your CV should carry sufficient eye-catching technical information relating to the job in question, but it should not be bogged down with it to the point where it defeats a lay-person's comprehension. It is important to try to second-guess the HR Department's selection criteria and aim to impress them initially. This particularly applies to criteria such as goal orientation, problem-solving and so on, which are required in some measure in virtually every job; that is why the PSP system especially emphasises a range of general competencies in every job application.

After this first sift, the line manager will usually be supplied with a selection of CVs for potentially good candidates. He or she will be particularly looking for initial evidence of how well you deliver the functions of the actual job, teamworking ability, how long you tend to stay in posts, and skills or experience that could add value to the team. Your CV therefore has to feature such points in good measure; the concept of analysing the *Key Competencies Required* in the actual job specifically addresses this need.

Within smaller companies, of course, there may not be a separate personnel department and the manager will deal with job applications directly. This is where HR and technical factors meet and are embodied in one person. However, that same manager may also be aware of the need to resolve organisational versus departmental conflicts (the attraction of a brilliant worker with a prickly personality may have to be weighed against the possible disruptive influence in a small team, for example). The actual administrative steps will still be rather similar in a smaller company but the process is somewhat simplified for the job-getter because it is not so important to consider and accommodate the differing internal politics of HR professionals and line management.

The line manager's wish list

The first task of the line manager is to draw up a list of responsibilities for the post. This is sometimes a fairly rough list but it may be a detailed job description (which later becomes part of the terms and conditions of employment). In a large-scale organisation, a job description will probably already exist but if not the line manager will consult with the personnel department to draw up a suitable document. A typical job description is shown in Figure 5.1. As you can see, this is conveniently sorted into short, sharp key points.

Figure 5.1 A typical job description

HGI plc

Job Title:
PROPERTY ADMINISTRATIVE OFFICER

Job Purpose:
To maintain all Property Records and Systems and provide full administrative and clerical support for the Estates Manager and the Valuers.

Main Responsibilities:
Inputting data to the property file records systems, including identifying and extracting relevant information from legal documents and files. Updating of records as necessary.

Assisting with the updating and maintaining of the map-based Whereabouts system, showing the organisation's land and property ownership.

Dealing with public and internal enquiries.

Monitoring the payment of rents.

Monitoring rent arrears situations. Initiating follow-up action with tenant, either by letter or by telephone. Making appointments for tenants with rent arrears to be interviewed by the Valuers, and following up agreed payment arrangements.

Maintaining a manual register of vacant property.

Preparing lettings particulars and circulating to applicants, accompanying on viewings, taking up references, etc. Maintaining a waiting list of applicants.

Organising the administration of management meetings, including taking minutes.

All general administrative and clerical functions.

Providing emergency cover for receptionist in the event of sickness, holidays, etc.

In the example used here, HGI plc is a medium-scale development and property organisation situated in a provincial town. One of its activities concerns the management and letting of rented property which is situated throughout the area. The property manager is seeking someone to handle the administrative and clerical work for this side of the business. The job description has been drawn up by the property manager and the human resources manager.

The job description, as the term implies, concerns the details of the *job*. However, recruitment is about the *people* who are going to fill the jobs. The line manager usually has an idea of the kind of person he or she wants to fill the position: extrovert or introvert, 'broad-brush' approach or more detail-oriented, and so on. Often, a formal person specification will also be drawn up (local authorities are particularly keen on them). The person specification shown in Figure 5.2 refers to the same role outlined by the job specification in Figure 5.1.

On the other hand, it may be just a 'wish list' scribbled on the back of an envelope. The following list is applicable to the HBI job vacancy:

- Lively and friendly personality with excellent communication skills

- Good character and honest – able to handle money accurately

- Good general clerical skills

- Able to work on own initiative with a minimum of supervision

- Smartly presented

- Computer literate with experience of using databases.

Figure 5.2 Person specification

	Essential	Desirable
Education and training	Good general education.	
Relevant experience	Administration of computer records. General administrative and clerical. Dealing with the public. Taking responsibility for own day-to-day workload. Working with computers.	Dealing with legal records. Property-related work. Budgets/invoicing using Sage Accounts. Access database.
Knowledge	Administrative systems.	Estates management and property procedures.
Skills and abilities	Organisational skills. Good keyboard skills. Good communication skills, both written and oral. Numerate.	Interpretation of property records and legal documents. Able to understand Ordnance Survey maps, using scales.

The job advertisement

When the job description has been established, the HR manager will use the information to prepare an advertisement.

Figure 5.3 shows an advertisement based on the job description and person specifications shown in Figures 5.1 and 5.2. This, of course, is the only information a potential applicant usually has about a vacant job, at least in the first instance. Any job application must usually be based solely on the content of the advertising copy so any other information that you can get – from a person with 'inside knowledge', for example – can be invaluable. In the absence of that, you have to rely on the advertisement itself, which, if you look for it, contains a wealth of vital information.

If the job and ideal person specifications have been used to draw up the advertisement, then obviously it is possible to analyse and disassemble the advertising copy to get back to that vital 'wish list'. Under the PSP system, the most important task is to identify and extricate the *Key Competencies Required* – the essential core skills of the job. Taking the advertisement, our aim is to work backwards, analysing the advertisement to produce an informed judgement on the 'wish list'. By doing this you can assemble a portfolio of core competencies that the employer requires in the ideal candidate.

The method of analysing job advertisements is examined in some detail later in this book, with more emphasis on 'essential', 'desirable' and other components. Briefly, the analysis involves taking the second or third viewpoints discussed earlier in this

---

Figure 5.3 Job advertisement

PROPERTY ADMINISTRATION OFFICER

Newtown   £17,000 to £18,500

An opportunity has arisen for someone to join our busy Estates Office as a Property Administration Officer.

The post involves taking responsibility for the control and administration of our extensive list of rented properties. This includes a wide range of administrative and clerical duties with an emphasis on computerised systems, and extensive liaison with members of the public.

The successful candidate will have a good general education and excellent communication skills. Experience of word processing and databases, managing efficient administrative systems and computer records is required. Must have the ability to use own initiative and work calmly and effectively under pressure.

Previous experience in Property Management, dealing with legal documents and property files would be an advantage. Knowledge of Microsoft Access and Sage Accounting packages would also be useful.

Written applications only, with a full CV, quoting reference EO131.

HGI

An Equal Opportunities Employer

Melody Carew, Human Resources Manager, HGI plc, The Walk Way, Newtown NN21 6QB

chapter – you 'think yourself' into the roles of the HR specialist recruiter and the line manager. The questions to ask are: 'Taking the wording of this advertisement, what clues are there to the thinking of the line manager?' And, 'What is behind the HR manager's specific terminology?'

Simply by taking a highlighter pen and marking relevant words in an advertisement, you will see how the story behind the copy begins to emerge. To demonstrate this, an analysis of the advertisement shown in Figure 5.3 would highlight the following points:

Essential qualities

- Responsibility

- Wide range of administrative and clerical duties

- Computerised systems

- Extensive liaison with members of the public

- Good general education

- Excellent communication skills

- Experience of word processing and database

- Administrative systems

- Computer records

- Work on own initiative

- Work calmly and effectively under pressure

Desirable characteristics

- Experience in property management

- Knowledge of Microsoft Access and Sage Accounting packages

- Dealing with legal documents and property files

Some factors will carry more weight than others, of course, but this is where you have to make an informed guess. As a general rule, err on the side of caution and include rather than exclude any identified points.

Looking at the list reveals that there is some overlap in the nature of the various factors. Indeed, many of them can be linked together in generic groups, as shown in Figure 5.4. It only remains to give a descriptive title to each generic group, and you will have successfully identified the *Key Competencies Required* at the heart of this job.

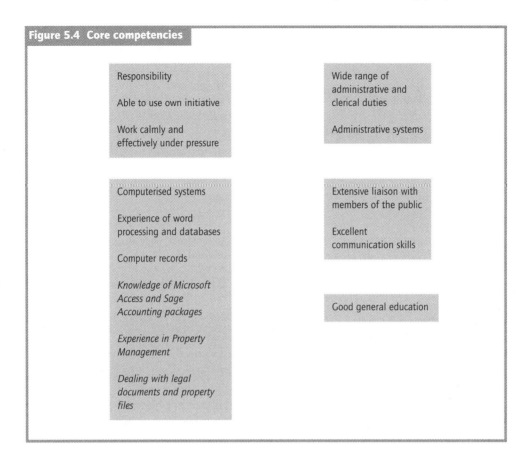

Figure 5.4 Core competencies

Responsibility

Able to use own initiative

Work calmly and
effectively under pressure

Wide range of
administrative and
clerical duties

Administrative systems

Computerised systems

Experience of word
processing and databases

Computer records

*Knowledge of Microsoft
Access and Sage
Accounting packages*

*Experience in Property
Management*

*Dealing with legal
documents and property
files*

Extensive liaison with
members of the public

Excellent
communication skills

Good general education

With practice, you will find that most job advertisements usually contain a recruiter's 'shopping list'. By looking at the second and third viewpoints, you will be better able to identify the needs and wishes of the recruiters. In later chapters we will look at how to take this approach still further to customise each and every individual job application to maximise your chances of success.

Chapter 6

Getting yourself organised

USE THIS CHAPTER TO PLAN, ORGANISE AND MANAGE YOUR JOB SEARCH ACTIVITIES.

Job-getting, like any task, can be made easier by efficient organisation and administration. It is an exercise in effective communication. Every message you send out gives a good or bad signal about yourself, not just by its content but, importantly, by its appearance, presentation and image. That is why companies spend colossal sums in achieving an effective corporate image and why they invest heavily in training their front-line staff in good customer relations skills.

Establishing an effective image for yourself need not cost you a fortune. It is largely a matter of setting and maintaining high standards, and much can be achieved with advance planning and forethought. Try to leave nothing to chance!

PLANNING YOUR JOB-SEARCH CAMPAIGN

Treat your job search as a major project. Planning, time management and self-discipline are essential features.

Employees who are under notice of dismissal by reason of redundancy should be given time off with pay for job-searching. This is set out in an ACAS Code of Practice. The amount of time that you may take off is not laid down, and the Code merely states that it must be 'reasonable'. There should be no problems regarding job interviews but time off for interview preparation may be questioned. You can argue that time off should also extend to visiting employment agencies, research trips to the local library, and so on. In the event of problems, get in touch with your nearest ACAS office for advice. ACAS Code of Practice booklets and contact details are available from any Jobcentre.

ORGANISING YOUR SCHEDULE

The aim is to provide you with a guide to planning an effective job-search campaign. A suggested schedule is provided in Figure 6.1. Notice that time has been allocated for leisure and/or keep-fit activities. Try not to confine your job-search to sitting at home, processing letters and application forms; that will make you feel very isolated and lonely if you are currently out of work. Get out and about, meet and talk to people, network, research magazines and papers at the library and try to lead an active social life.

Build in time for your leisure activities, and make sure that you keep this time for yourself. It is vital to your health and well-being. Above all, make a point of talking to people. Arrange meetings and network with your contacts. Involvement with Job Clubs, further education courses and support groups can be very beneficial.

Figure 6.1 Job search schedule

		Morning	Afternoon	Evening
Monday	09.30 am	Produce 5 speculative letters	Mail letters Study local newspaper ads	Produce applications for any suitable job ads
	11.00 am	Review Job Search diary Make follow-up phone calls		
Tuesday	09.30 am	Mail job applications Visit the Job Centre	Study local newspaper ads Telephone 5 companies	Produce applications for suitable job ads
	11.30 am	Input company names and addresses into your database	EXERCISE/LEISURE	
Wednesday	9.30 am	Produce 5 speculative letters	Study local newspaper ads Mail letters	Produce applications for suitable job ads
	11.00 am	Input company names and addresses into your database	Visit library	
Thursday	9.30 am	Visit Job Centre	Study local newspaper ads	
	11.30 am	Input company names and addresses into your database	Produce job applications	
Friday	9.30 am	Produce 5 speculative letters	EXERCISE/LEISURE	
	11.00 am	Input company names and addresses into your database		
Saturday				
Sunday				

Do it now

Using the blank timetable provided in Figure 6.2, organise your own programme to allow some flexibility for job interviews and other things that might arise in your life. Take some time now to plan a timetable that realistically suits your lifestyle. Set aside time for family and personal matters (taking children to school or visiting relatives and friends, for example). However, in general terms, plan a schedule and stick to it. Establish a routine to structure your day.

Include these tasks in your schedule:

- re-writing your career history – 4 hours
- producing your CV – 4 hours
- producing speculative letters – daily
- making follow-up phone calls – daily
- studying local newspaper ads – daily

Figure 6.2 Blank job search schedule

	Morning	Afternoon	Evening
Monday			
Tuesday			
Wednesday			
Thursday			
Friday			
Saturday			
Sunday			

▧ researching and inputting company names and addresses into your database – 3 to 4 hours a week

▧ visiting the Job Centre – twice a week

▧ visiting local library – once a week

▧ on-line research and job-search (if applicable) – daily

▧ producing job applications – daily.

You will need to plan your diary in order to make sure that nothing is missed out. The following elements must be accommodated:

▧ Identifying potential employers within your chosen job markets involves intensive research. Find employers' addresses to build your own employer database using:

  – trade directories

  – telephone directory

  – local authorities

  – chamber of commerce

  – Internet

  – newspapers and magazines

  – 'leg-work'.

▧ Effective researching also involves the simultaneous scouring and monitoring of the advertised job markets. This requires locating and regularly monitoring relevant sources of job advertisements such as:

  – newspapers and magazines

  – institute and trade journals

  – company and organisation vacancy bulletins

  – radio

  – Internet.

▧ Personal networking means mobilising your own personal contacts, both to gain personal referrals to employers and to obtain information on possible opportunities, managers' names, etc. This involves:

  – beginning and maintaining a personal contacts list

  – colleagues who now work for other employers

  – associates working with suppliers you have dealt with

  – representatives of customers and clients who know your work

- contacting trainers and tutors who have coached you in the past.

- professional bodies, institutes and trade unions

- friends and 'friends of friends'

- relatives

- visiting trade shows

- newsgroups on the Internet.

EQUIPMENT

Basic necessities

First, there are some obvious equipment requirements:

■ access to a telephone, preferably with an answer machine;

■ a means of producing documents, usually by personal computer (PC) and printer.

If you do not have these already then it is necessary to use some ingenuity to get the use of them. There is no way of doing without them. CVs and letters must be printed using a word processor and printer. Do not expect to rely with any success on photocopies or handwritten documents.

The actual ownership of an online computer and printer is not essential but it is certainly beneficial. It offers the following advantages:

■ immediate access and full control of your smartly presented letters and CVs;

■ the facility easily and quickly to customise your CV for specific job applications;

■ an efficient recording and filing system;

■ the ability to produce speculative letters to potential employers using mailmerge.

If you add a modem and a telephone connection to your home computer, you will be able access the Internet and receive e-mail. This is becoming increasingly important and the next chapter is devoted to the subject of online resources.

Even if you do not have a computer you can make arrangements with accommodating friends or use an office services bureau. Some employment agencies will also produce your letters and CVs for a price. You can access the Internet at computer terminals in public libraries and the increasingly numerous Internet cafes.

Stationery

Time to go shopping! You will need:

- an A4 notepad

- two A4 size loose-leaf files

- polythene filing wallets

- A4 100 g/m² smooth paper (white or cream)

- A4 size, self-sealing envelopes (preferably white, 'window' envelopes)

- postage stamps

- paper clips.

The telephone

Many employers prefer to make an initial contact by telephone rather than writing letters. Cultivate a good telephone manner, adopting a businesslike but not overly formal approach.

Use your first name or the one you are usually known by: 'This is Mike Smith speaking' is much better than 'This is Mr Smith speaking'. You will notice that many recruiters give their first names in job advertisements and it is certainly a more friendly approach.

If you are living away, then make sure that you obtain some message-taking service that is accessible by remote access. The BT Callminder service and many modern answering machines offer this facility.

> Try to ensure quiet privacy in the room where your telephone is situated. A background noise of dogs barking or children screeching will not help your self-marketing image.

Files

You will need loose-leaf files and polythene filing wallets so that you can keep copies of the various record sheets you will be using with the PSP system. You also need to keep a copy of your library resource CV and copies of any specifically tailored CVs that you send out in response to job advertisements.

You will need to keep copies of job advertisements, the letters you write and application forms you complete, as well as CVs you send. The essence of the Globeskills system is that you will be making targeted approaches to employers and you will need to know exactly what you said or wrote in each particular case when you are contacted in reply.

Paper

Always use good quality A4 (210 × 297 mm), 100 g/m^2 paper. Don't use cheap, flimsy photocopy paper and never send hand-written letters scrawled on ruled writing pads.

You should opt for white, ivory or cream paper which denotes good taste and style. It is usually more economical if you buy a box of 500 sheets, and you will need this sort of quantity to use the system described in this book. However, smaller packs are usually available if necessary.

Use this paper for your CVs and for your letters. Don't produce more than a dozen copies of your CV at any one time, unless you have a specific purpose for them. You will often need to change the content or layout for specific job applications.

Envelopes

Never fold your CV or the accompanying letter. Again, it is a matter of good presentation. You should aim for your documents to arrive on the recruiter's desk in pristine condition. Your application will look particularly smart when placed alongside others from people who have folded and scrunched up their paperwork. Always use an envelope that will accept an A4 unfolded sheet – white is preferably but manila is acceptable.

It is a good idea to use envelopes with a transparent window for the address (these are available in A4 size). With a little practice you can produce your letters so that the recipient's address is in the right position. This assists in good presentation, and it saves a considerable amount of time when you are sending out many applications.

When sending a letter to a named manager you should always endorse the envelope 'Private and Confidential', using neat bold lettering or a rubber stamp. This is particularly effective with speculative applications because it usually ensures that the envelope is presented to the manager unopened. Otherwise, an overly-officious secretary or administrative worker might 'filter out' such correspondence.

TIME TO BEGIN IN EARNEST

Having prepared yourself, committed your time and organised your equipment and stationery, it is time to commence your job search to achieve a brilliant new future.

Chapter 7

Using a computer and online resources

MANY PEOPLE HAVE ACCESS TO A PERSONAL COMPUTER WITH AN INTERNET CONNECTION. WHILST IT ISN'T ESSENTIAL TO YOUR JOB SEARCH ACTIVITIES, IT IS CERTAINLY A GREAT BENEFIT. THIS CHAPTER GIVES VALUABLE INFORMATION ABOUT JOB SITES AND ON-LINE JOB SEARCHING.

A comprehensive book dealing with job searching in the twenty-first century simply cannot ignore the Internet. Not everyone has access to a personal computer (PC), of course, and it is certainly possible to mount an effective job-search without one. However, there are great benefits to be had in using online resources and many public libraries offer PC facilities and you can also use internet cafes.

To discuss matters such as Internet Service Providers (ISPs) and equipment is beyond the scope of this book. Suffice it to say that you don't need the most advanced and expensive computer to access the Internet. Indeed, virtually any type of computer manufactured in the last 15 years will enable you to surf the Net, providing that you have some sort of modem to connect it to the telephone system. New, low-spec computers are relatively cheap nowadays and they are perfectly adequate, not only for Internet use but also as a word processing and information storage tool.

This chapter, then, is intended for those people who own or have access to a personal computer (PC). It is devoted to providing details of use of the most effective use of the Internet as a means of:

- searching for job vacancy advertisements;
- distributing your CV;
- finding job-search support services, i.e. CV writing and skills analysis;
- researching for company and sector information.

WHAT IS THE INTERNET?

The Internet, also known as the Net, is the world's largest computer network. Put more simply, it is a network of several networks, linking millions of separate computers that are somehow electronically hooked up together to share information and services. Some of the main services are:

- e-mail – electronic mail;

- information retrieval;

- e-commerce – electronic buying and selling;

- newsgroups;

- intranets – networks used for internal communications by companies and organisations;

- communications – Internet Relay Chat, a multi-user party line for real-time text chat with people all over the world.

Using the Internet at any time of night and day is an easy and fast medium for job-hunting, giving instant access to recruitment agencies. Also, it is probably the most efficient and economical way to seek out job vacancy advertisements from newspapers (most maintain a website), and many companies own web pages which feature a jobs section. You can make instant applications with many recruiters via e-mail, literally at the touch of a button. It offers a way to send your CV to as many agencies and companies as possible. The Internet is therefore growing increasingly important in the job-hunter's tools.

However, a word of warning: avoid the temptation to become totally absorbed with this medium to the exclusion of other, more traditional methods. This is particularly important advice for people who are already familiar with the Internet and who tend to rely upon it in many areas of their lives. It is tempting to use this seemingly painless and non-taxing method rather than tackling the admitted grind of sending out letters of application by ordinary mail. The fact is, though, that only 5 per cent of jobs are actually recruited via the Internet. This merely puts it into perspective and it does not mean that you should ignore online resources.

THE WORLD WIDE WEB AND SEARCH ENGINES

The World Wide Web is nothing more nor less than a giant database of millions of websites across the world. Each of these sites is dedicated to some specific purpose, whether it be commercial, community-driven or private, and they all combine text, sound, pictures and, increasingly, animation to get their message across. The Web lets you roam (surf) to your heart's content, seeking out interesting information and services. The problem is that there is so much stuff out there that it can be utterly overwhelming. It is almost impossible to find relevant sites and information without tools such as search engines.

A search engine is a free online service that finds the things you are seeking. There are several different ones, of varying types. The following search engines are very comprehensive and easy to use:

- http://www.Google.com

- http://Yahoo.com

If you want to use other engines, a very convenient way is to access http://www.Dogpile.co.uk. This is known as a 'meta-search' and it uses the results from several of the other search engines with web and UK-only search. Give it a try, and you will probably be amazed at its ease of use.

To access a search engine

1. Link into the Internet via your modem and start your web browser (usually Internet Explorer or Netscape).

2. Type in the web addresses of the search engine's home page.

3. If, as is usual, a Search box is offered, type some carefully chosen keywords into the box and click Search.

It is as easy as that. The engine will search its huge database and turn up a list of sites based on your keywords. However, the list is likely to be immense. If you typed in keywords such as 'jobs', 'employment', 'recruitment agencies', 'employers' and so on, you will have a positive deluge of suggested sites.

That is where 'gateway sites' are particularly useful to your job-search activities.

GATEWAYS

A gateway site is a portal to other relevant sites. It is, in fact, a site that specialises in a particular subject area and all of the search work has already been done for you. Teams of researchers and programmers have evaluated, sorted, organised and presented all the relevant information into indexes, and they usually provide links to take you directly to the sites you choose from among their lists.

These portals provide a logical and easy method of accessing all kinds of job search information and services. Through them, you can get help in writing and preparing your CV and, when you are satisfied with the content and presentation, you may distribute it to recruiters. You can also get good advice on all kinds of topics, ranging from pensions to legal matters. Job vacancy listings are presented in an easy to use form, with access to electronic newspaper advertisements. The gateway sites listed below might be all that you will need. Save the web addresses in a special folder in the Favourites or Bookmark feature of your browser for ease of access.

- www.careers.org/index.html. This is a particularly good international site with a comprehensive UK section. Also, of course, it can be ideal if you are considering relocation to another country. It offers over 8,000 links to jobs, employers, newspapers, career and recruitment professionals, colleges, libraries… this is a very comprehensive organised listing service.

- uk.careers.yahoo.com/. This is a site offered in conjunction with the Yahoo! search engine. It is an excellent and comprehensive site, offering all kinds of career services.

- www.job-page.co.uk. This covers UK job sites and international sites with a UK focus, and it also offers several other useful links including CV help and distribution sites.

- www.lifestyle.co.uk. This site links to over 500 job sites, some of which offer CV registration and distribution.

- www.jobs.co.uk. This is a portal that provides its own useful job-search tools.

NEWSPAPER SITES

Local and national newspapers usually keep their own websites with a jobs section that lists all advertised vacancies featured in its pages. The site for your local newspaper can be found by using a search engine. The following national sites are recommended:

- www.Appointments-plus.co.uk. This site is for *The Daily Telegraph* job pages.

- www.jobsunlimited.co.uk. This is probably the best newspaper site, listing every job vacancy advertised in *The Guardian* every week.

- www.thetimes-appointments.co.uk. This site gives all the jobs from *The Times* and *The Sunday Times*.

JOB SITES

There are literally thousands of job sites on the Net so it is necessary to focus your activities. The following sites are recommended to the online job searcher:

- www.topjobs.co.uk. This site is a bit cumbersome but offers both UK and international vacancies.

- www.monster.co.uk. This site is easy to use, with both UK and overseas positions.

- www.cityjobs.com. This site covers the financial, IT and media sectors. The site monitors your visit and saves details of your career interests to e-mail relevant vacancies to you automatically.

- www.futurestep.co.uk. Use this site to register your candidacy for management and executive level positions.

- www.jobshark.com. This site includes UK and overseas positions. Major company profiles are available.

- www.pricejam.com. This site offers media and communications related jobs.

- www.Careermosiac.com

- www.Jobpilot.com

- www.Datumeurope.com

- www.BigBlueDog.com

- www.fish4jobs.co.uk

The above sites offer good general management vacancies in the UK.

- www.job-channel.com. This is a nice user-friendly site for both permanent and temporary posts.

- www.totaljobs.co.uk. This site offers good general management vacancies in the UK, is quick and easy and has a CV registration service.

- www.fiftyon.co.uk. Many people over 50 years of age worry about their prospects in job markets, despite modern claims that '50 is the new 30'. This website is for those aged 50 plus. It tends to concentrate on executive and general management vacancies, but also often has interim assignments.

- www.workthing.com. This site has lots of features and general vacancies.

- www.jobsjobsjobs.co.uk. This site perhaps has too many jobs for your liking as you will have to look at all vacancies in the required geographical location, rather than search by job category. There are plenty of jobs here, though.

- www.good4jobs.co.uk. This site offers permanent and contract work.

- www.peoplebank.co.uk. This site, again, offers both permanent and contract work.

This is not an exclusive list, of course, and you can add your own favourite sites as you find them.

CV REGISTRATION AND DISTRIBUTION SERVICES

The great advantage of the Internet is the scope for interaction and, quite literally, networking of your information. A key feature of Internet job-search is the availability of CV registration and CV distribution services. Note, the distinction between the two:

- CV registration entails submitting your CV with details of job interests and the site then notifies you of relevant job opportunities by e-mail.

- CV distribution is a service whereby a site sends your CV to as many other sites, recruitment agencies and employers as possible.

Many websites offer a service whereby you register an electronic version of your CV on their database, either just for registration or for distribution too. To aid the site's information storage and retrieval functions, the CV is sometimes a stylised version derived from a questionnaire, although others will accept your own document.

If you opt for a CV distribution service, then choose one that will give the most appropriate targeted approach rather than blanket coverage. Remember that you are responsible for your own CV and what happens to it. By definition, your CV contains many private details, including name, address and an indication of lifestyle. You should always check exactly what the site will be doing with your personal information. Look at the privacy policy in each case.

It is particularly important to research companies thoroughly before attending an interview resulting from an online job search. Talk to them on the phone if in any doubt, and exercise sensible caution. This advice is important, particularly but not exclusively, for women and young people.

SOME CV REGISTRATION AND DISTRIBUTION SITES

The following sites do not charge a fee for registering your CV online with other sites/agencies and potential employers.

- www.Appointments-plus.co.uk

- www.BigBlueDog.com

- www.businessfile.co.uk

- www.fiftyon.co.uk

- www.Jobpilot.com

- www.jobserve.co.uk

- www.jobsunlimited.co.uk

- www.monster.co.uk

- www.newmonday.com

- www.pricejam.com

- www.reed.co.uk

- www.workthing.com

RECRUITMENT AGENCIES ON THE NET

The Internet is an ideal medium for recruitment agencies and some of them advertise jobs from many other sites too. Most of these are easily found and accessed through the gateway sites listed earlier in this chapter. You can also log onto the Recruitment and Employment Confederation portal site:

- www.rec.uk.com

This site provides a wide range of information on recruitment agencies and also offers consultancy-finding services.

INFORMATION AND RESEARCH

Besides locating job vacancies, the Internet offers very sophisticated and easy-to-use tools for finding information. You should always research a company before making a job application, and suitably target your self-marketing materials. Also, many companies have their own websites with jobs pages, and you can find out such site addresses with some intelligent searching.

The following sites are good for researching a specific company or industrial sector, and you should bookmark them on your browser.

- www.dnb.co.uk

- www.kellys.co.uk

- www.kompass.co.uk

These are complex and huge directories of companies, suppliers, manufacturers and merchants. They are a little daunting to use but contain a wealth of information.

Usenet

Usenet is an Internet system that provides forums for ordinary people (users) gathered in thousands of separate interest groups, known as newsgroups. In other words, they are like bulletin boards, where users can post their own messages and read and, if so inclined, reply to those posted by others. You will need a newsreader progam to access the newsgroups, and these are available free of charge; Forte Free Agent is particularly good and is obtainable by downloading from the Internet, or from free CD-ROMs supplied by many computer-dedicated magazines. You can also use Microsoft Outlook or Outlook Express newsreaders, among others. The list of available Newsgroups varies, depending on your Internet Service Provider. Try the following:

- free.uk.jobs

- uk.jobs

- uk.jobs.offered

- uk.jobs.wanted

Discovering trends

Additionally, you might like to browse through a site that offers inside-track information on employment trends and likely areas of future job opportunities:

- www.ukbusinesspark.co.uk

The DTI has a wealth of useful information on a wide range of issues affecting people at work:

- http://www.dti.gov.uk/for_employees.html

In particular, take a look at the Employment Market Analysis And Research (Emar) page. This provides advice on employment relations and labour markets. It is supported by an ongoing programme of evaluation and research, assesses the impact of particular policies or regulations and examines emergent trends:

- http://www.dti.gov.uk/er/emar/index.htm

Finally, don't forget the Jobcentre Plus website. This has had a real makeover in recent times and offers a wealth of information and advice with some good job search tools, too:

- http://www.jobcentreplus.gov.uk/

Chapter 8 ■

Rewriting your career history

THE PURPOSE OF THIS CHAPTER IS TO MAKE AN INVENTORY OF THE VARIOUS COMPO-
NENTS THAT MIGHT BE INCLUDED IN YOUR PACKAGE OF *PRIME SELLING POINTS* THAT
YOU WILL OFFER TO EMPLOYERS.

What can you offer to other employers? What are your *Prime Selling Points*? Under
the Globeskills PSP system you will offer selected skills and qualities bundled in a
package that is specifically tailored to the needs of the target job every time. Of
course, the bundle will be somewhat different for each job application. The purpose
of this chapter is to make an inventory of the various components that might be
included in any given bundle of *Prime Selling Points*.

INVENTORY OF SKILLS AND EXPERIENCE

You have already done some serious work in analysing and auditing your skills and
attributes. This is now taken a stage further by looking at each of your jobs and
seeing where the skills were gathered and used. The process is divided into two
parts:

1. Writing up your employment history.

2. Making a job record for each position that you have held, analysing each job and
   drawing out your skills, experience and achievements, etc.

The task in hand is to identify and list the various aspects of your skills, experience
and attributes, and organise your records in a way that makes them readily accessible when you need them. The method used here is to structure your records around
a chronological career history: working backwards, each job that you have done is
taken in turn, analysing and extracting the various skills, achievements and aptitudes demonstrated in that role.

The inventory will be used to provide suitable material for your CVs and self-marketing letters. It will also be a handy reference when you fill in application forms,

having already gathered all the information you will need. Later, of course, it will be useful for your interview preparation, too.

In producing this inventory, there are three main requirements:

▨   list all of your various attributes;

▨   provide evidence;

▨   present the evidence in a structured manner.

Complete this important part of your job-getting project carefully and you will reap the benefit many times over. It will become your ready-reference source of information when applying for jobs and save you having to repeat the work when processing each new job application.

PREPARING YOUR EMPLOYMENT HISTORY

First, build a summary of your employment history using the chart in Figure 8.1. You need only provide brief details. This will later be used for supplying information to a prospective employer, so give it a positive slant.

Figure 8.1 Employment history

List your jobs in *reverse chronological* order providing *brief* details

Date started	Date left	Employer		Job title		Brief job description
		Turnover				
		Nature of business		Starting salary	Leaving salary	Reason for leaving
		Turnover				
		Nature of business		Starting salary	Leaving salary	Reason for leaving
		Turnover				
		Nature of business		Starting salary	Leaving salary	Reason for leaving

The summary provides a useful reference source when making job applications, besides gathering information for your CV. So, although this is an exercise about you rather than about past employers, it is a good idea to make the effort and organise the information that is commonly required on application forms. Some of the information is useful for your own purposes: for instance, company turnover can illustrate scale and add weight to your employment history. Begin by listing your jobs in *reverse chronological order*.

Employment record

- List the month/year of starting and leaving for each period of employment.
- Include dates of periods of unemployment.

Details about the employer

You should note details of:

- the employer's address;
- the nature of the business (e.g. food wholesaler and distributor).
- a broad estimate of turnover, either of the branch, depot, business unit or entire group (if unknown, this can often be obtained from trade directories such as *Key British Enterprises* or *Kompas* which are available at most public libraries.)

Job title and other details

When taking up references, prospective employers often seek confirmation of the title of the job you occupied; it is therefore advisable to list the formal job title on application forms. This is not necessarily the case with your CV, however. Many formal job titles are sometimes misleading and owe more to creativity by employers than to an accurate reflection of the job itself. It is sometimes best to choose a more appropriate and descriptive title for your CV.

List the formal title of the most senior post you held under each company, and a more descriptive title if appropriate. Remember to list separate jobs with a single employer, showing career progression with dates. Finally, add details of your starting and leaving salary.

For periods of unemployment

Where possible, give some details to explain and mitigate each period of unemployment as in the following examples:

'Bringing up a young family, during which I helped to found and run a local playgroup.'

'Undertook voluntary work for local Community Centre, installing electrical circuits.'

Reason for leaving

A separate space has been provided on our form for this question, and it frequently appears on application forms. Work out a formula of words for each job that you have held. Bear in mind that this is your preparation for responses that you may give to an employer, so it is unwise to state anything too damning (you simply would not get an interview). Bland statements such as 'Career advancement' or 'To broaden experience' are good standbys.

COMPILING YOUR JOB RECORDS

For the second part of this exercise you need to think carefully about each of the jobs listed in your employment history. Using a separate job record sheet for each job like the one shown in Figure 8.2, list all of the duties that you carried out and the experience that you achieved. If you have a long history with one organisation, use a separate sheet for each identifiable period of your career.

Note that 'duties' and 'experience' are not one and the same thing. You are not trying to recreate the employer's job description. It is more than likely that you gained valuable experience in something that was not part of your formal job description, but which you did nevertheless (deputising for the supervisor, for example), and it is the sort of achievement that you should highlight.

Remember that these records provide the raw material for your future self-marketing campaigns. You will offer this material in tailored packages, with two elements:

- selected *Prime Selling Points* (the specific functions and attributes that you have identified as being particularly important for the specific job);

- a number of general competencies: those general skills such as communications, teamworking, goal orientation, etc., each of which is applicable to all jobs in greater or lesser measure.

These then are the items that need to be teased out from any period of employment. You are looking for skills and experience nuggets that can be used later for your PSP bundles. This is also an essential part of preparing a winning and effective CV. The experience and skills you identify here will be added to your personal library of marketing points which you can draw upon when putting together effective job applications.

This exercise compels you to take a fresh look at your employment record and review it from a different perspective. The aim here is to view your work history with an eye on where you now want to go rather than where you have already been. Again, you should consider the second and third viewpoints referred to in previous chapters, asking yourself how the recruiters would view the information. Of course,

Figure 8.2 Job record sheet		
Employer:		Starting date:
Job title		Leaving date:

Main achievements and experience

KEY POINTS

Communications

Organisational skills

Goal orientation

Integrity

Problem-solving

Teamworking

Summary of purpose/responsibilities of job

you should not fabricate untruths. You obviously cannot change things that have already occurred. What you are now seeking to bring out are your tangible skills, experience and attributes which can ultimately be used to demonstrate your ability to match the *Key Competencies Required* of the job you now seek.

It is a question of carefully analysing the skills you acquired and demonstrated in each job that you have held; too many people do not properly understand just how valuable these skills are. The aim here is to review your pool of experience. Careful consideration of each job that you have held in the past is valuable preparation for producing an effective CV. It is also an essential exercise in knowing yourself and preparing for future interviews.

Main achievements and experience

When asked to prepare an employment history, many people concentrate on providing employers' names, job titles and lists of responsibilities. These are fine as far as they go, but they say nothing about a person's achievements or attributes.

So, what kind of information is likely to tempt a recruiter to buy your skills and experience? He or she will probably not be too excited by the fact that you once were a process engineer supervising seven junior engineers or an electrical fitter working within a maintenance team of a large factory. These kinds of facts say a lot about the job but nothing about you. You should aim for statements that will lead the employer to think, 'If this person could achieve that for Acme Products, he or she could achieve similar things for my company too'.

Your specific skills are particularly important, as is any valuable experience that you may have. But you should also include special talents or attributes that you possess and which are particularly relevant to the target (e.g. a head for heights would be especially important in a job dealing with overhead power lines).

So, look first at the main achievements and experience section, and seek to find informative pen-pictures to describe your achievements in the job. The following are examples of some winning statements:

> *'Successfully developed a new system for separating nitrogen from air, improving measurable efficiency by 15 per cent, and improving profits by £80,000 per annum.'*

> *'Designed and implemented a planned preventative maintenance schedule, reducing machine downtime by 30 per cent.'*

> *'Identified and investigated customer services problems within the store, implementing a targeted training programme which resulted in a 50 per cent reduction in customer complaints.'*

> *'Analysed workload and prioritised own working schedules to maximise efficiency and consistently exceed productivity targets.'*

Just consider the above statements for a few seconds. Each of them uses strong proactive words: *identified, resolved, analysed, designed, implemented*. These give a strong sense of dynamic action. Each statement starts by stating what the person actually did and follows this with a bold claim of the benefits that this action gained for the company. Implicit within every such statement is a promise to gain similar benefits on behalf of another employer.

Many people have difficulty in recognising their own achievements. Think in terms of benefits. In this context, anything that gave a benefit to an employer is an achievement. You can identify your achievements by asking:

- What was the employer's purpose in placing you in that particular job?

- What did the company gain by employing you?

- If you had not been in the job, what things would not have happened?

Other questions to ask are:

- Did managers, customers or colleagues pass any favourable comments about you and, if so, what did you do that impressed them?

- Were you selected for any particular tasks? What were they, and how well did you do the jobs?

Supplement your achievements with details of any skill developed during this period of employment (an achievement in its own right, of course) This same structure also accommodates examples that demonstrate your various aptitudes and general attributes (e.g. self-motivation and enthusiasm).

General competencies

The PSP system includes a carefully selected battery of general competencies. Having looked at the specific achievements and skills of the job, now take some time to try to find similar statements which demonstrate your ability under each of the headings listed below. Probably, some of the achievements that you have already selected will fit the bill perfectly. Try to find other examples, however, as this will further strengthen the case. The idea is to find an effective illustration for each of the separate competencies within each of your jobs – or, at any rate, your most recent ones. The various general competency exercises featured throughout this book are designed to help you find effective answers.

- *Communications*. Try to find an example or examples within the job which demonstrate good communication skills.

- *Organisational skills*. Choose some telling bullet points that show your ability to use a methodical approach to organisational matters.

- *Goal orientation*. Give evidence of setting yourself goals and using determination to achieve them.

- *Integrity*. You must show a professional approach that does not compromise or trade off high standards.

- *Problem-solving*. Give examples where you identified, investigated and resolved difficulties, preferably including some indication of scale (i.e. cash sum saved, profit increased, etc).

- *Teamworking*. Show that you encouraged others, promoted a good working environment, or motivated a team to achieve some objective.

There will be occasions when one of the general competencies is so important to a particular job that it will be elevated in status. In the main, however, they will be the supporting cast for your star performers of *Prime Selling Points*. This is a matter of judgement when identifying the *Key Competencies Required* for any given job.

SUMMARY

When you have completed these exercises, you will have an employment history which summarises your career, supplemented by a separate job record sheet for each role. These roles will be either within one company or in different periods of employment. The employment history and job record sheets provide the following:

- a record of your employment history, complete with dates and job titles – this will be used for your CV and for application forms;

- a summary of the purpose of each job – this will be used in your CV, in application forms and also when answering questions when telephone canvassing and at interviews;

- a list of bullet points which summarise your achievements, skills, experience and attributes demonstrated in that particular role – this will be used in compiling your *Prime Selling Points* bundles and will also provide the material for your CVs, self-marketing letters and application forms.

- practical examples which demonstrate how well you meet the criteria of general competencies – one or other of these examples might be used as a *Prime Selling Point* when it is particularly important in a given job. However, they will generally be used to show a 'rounded' and employable character and will therefore feature in all of your CVs and self-marketing material.

Chapter 9

Considering CVs

THIS CHAPTER OUTLINES THE KEY PRINCIPLES IN PRODUCING A WINNING CV.

'There are nine and sixty ways of constructing tribal lays and every single one of them is right.'

Rudyard Kipling.

Curriculum vitae is a Latin term which, loosely-translated, means 'the course of life'. It is more commonly abbreviated to 'CV', and means a brief account of one's previous occupations, education and qualifications. There is no 'right' way to compile a CV but some presentations make greater impact than others.

This is an important chapter that should not be skipped as it discusses the various issues to be considered in producing an effective self-marketing document. It outlines the key principles, and signposts common mistakes that should be avoided.

THE PURPOSE OF A CV

It is commonly said that your CV is the most important single document in your job search. However, this is not entirely correct. An essential point of the PSP system is that you do not rely upon a single CV which you hope will somehow magically cater for every purpose. Each CV that you send out is carefully tailored to the specific job application. This may mean changing the content, the presentation or even the whole format, depending upon the needs of the occasion. Usually, however, it is convenient to write a 'standard' CV and amend it according to need. That is the approach used here.

Certain items have to be included of course, no matter what format or general material you use. Your document should contain the following information about you:

- name and address;

- home telephone number, mobile telephone number and e-mail address (if applicable);

▦ employment history;

▦ education, qualifications and vocational training;

▦ personal details – date of birth, marital status, etc.;

▦ Leisure interests.

> **Your CV cannot get you the job on its own. It is a marketing tool. The product that it advertises is *you*.**

Another misconception is that the sole purpose of your CV is to obtain an interview. This simplistic approach serves a purpose in focusing the mind, of course: the CV is to obtain an interview, and the interview is to obtain the job. But CVs have various other functions. They have become marketing documents aimed at positioning your own particular skills and experience package in job markets. Preparing, producing and placing the document is a valuable skills analysis and self-marketing exercise in its own right.

A well-written and focused CV can also prepare the ground for a successful interview, which is a wholly more ambitious project than merely aiming for an invitation to attend. 'Talk me through your CV' is a common request at interviews. In these circumstances, an all-purpose CV is 'hit and miss' at best, whereas a targeted marketing document will unerringly direct the recruiter's line of questioning to your *Prime Selling Points*.

Skilful wording and prioritisation can therefore 'pull' the interviewer onto territory where you are particularly strong and divert attention from less attractive aspects. On the other hand, a carelessly written CV can be a hostage to fortune because a skilful interviewer will investigate the significance of both inclusions and omissions. As any experienced recruiter knows, a CV is particularly eloquent in the things it does not say. You must therefore try to ensure that your document takes account of every important angle. A significant omission can be costly: the question can take up valuable interview time even if you have an answer ready to rectify it.

> **An important aim of any CV (or any part of a job application) is *not* to invite a potentially negative line of questioning.**

Contrary to usual advice, judiciously used professional jargon can strike a chord of empathy with another fellow-professional, invoking a feeling that 'he or she is one of us'.

Your 'reserve' CV material can form part of a viable interview 'script'. This is a particularly valid point when using the PSP system and constantly revising and amending your various offerings. When asked questions at interviews, you will find that you have a fund of ready answers in your mind, deriving from your library of selling points which have not necessarily been emphasised in the particular job application. This is all part of the holistic and rounded nature of PSP which, taken as a whole, provides a coherent system whereby any single component assists in all other areas of your job-getting activity.

An effective CV, then, performs a variety of useful and, indeed, vital functions. Rather than your CV being the single most important document in your job search, the ability to produce effective and winning CVs is probably the most important part of your job-getting system.

APPEALING TO RECRUITERS' DIFFERING AGENDAS

In every aspect of preparing your CV you should take the second and third viewpoints referred to in previous chapters and ask yourself the following questions:

- 'If I were the HR recruiter selecting a person for this interview, what points would I be looking for?'

    and…

- 'If I were the line manager requiring someone to do this job in my department, what points would I be looking for?'

This approach takes account of the potentially differing priorities of HR/personnel specialists and line managers. Remember, though, that the HR /personnel specialists will probably make the *initial* selection of likely candidates and they will not necessarily be impressed by or even understand masses of technical information. On the other hand, they will appreciate a CV that demonstrates good general competencies and pass it to task-oriented line managers, who *will* want to see more detailed technical information. You must therefore strike a balance between these conflicting needs.

A good rule is to produce a CV which provides an attractive 'broad-brush' immediate impact to please the HR specialist, backed up with sufficient technical detail, less prominently displayed, to satisfy a discriminating line manager.

Think of an advertising leaflet: a sausage will be marketed as a 'wholesome aromatic banger sizzling in the pan', with evocative, eye-catching images attractively displayed; the list of ingredients and supporting details will be discretely shown in a much less prominent position. You should organise your CV along similar lines.

YOUR ACHIEVEMENTS EQUAL EMPLOYERS' BENEFITS

This book has already highlighted the need to concentrate upon your achievements. For the purposes of your CV you should view *achievements* in the context of *benefits* that you have brought to an employer. Further, a distinction is drawn between *potential benefits* on the one hand, and *features* on the other.

The 'So what?' test will help to illustrate and separate the two concepts:

Q 'What is the product?'

A 'The PSP job-getting system.'

Q 'OK. What is its feature?'

A 'PSP is an integrated system which matches the specific needs of the job and your best selling points.'

Q 'So what?'

A 'You are more likely to get the job because you focus at all times on the things that are important to the recruiter and make best use of every opportunity to succeed rather than wasting time and effort on irrelevant matters.'

From your career point of view, you can apply this simple 'so what? test' to any single item for your CV.

'I developed a new mail distribution and collation method for the company.'

'*So what?*'

'It enabled a speedier response to customer orders and resulted in an average reduction of one day in delivery turnaround time, contributing to an increase of £118,000 in annual sales.'

Again, the last response is the 'benefit' (note too the judicious use of the phrase 'contributing to…' which enables you to claim a part of team achievements in all honesty). Once you have analysed your achievements in this way it is not difficult to rephrase the final paragraph to present a very persuasive and attractive selling point. Note that benefits are more powerfully illustrated by providing some scale or notion of quantity, usually expressed in terms of a cash sum saved, percentage gains and so on. Try to add this kind of detail to your achievements as a matter of course.

HR/personnel specialists tend to buy potential benefits for the organisation as a whole (fulfilling their role in developing and maintaining a multi-functional workforce within company policies), while line managers mainly buy potential benefits for the departmental unit (fulfilling their role in running an efficient productive unit without avoidable problems). Put more crudely, and perhaps controversially,

HR/personnel people recruit for the organisation and line managers recruit for themselves. Importantly, though, both of them buy potential benefits and not features.

Job titles, duties and responsibilities are merely features. Potential benefits are illustrated through your achievements. Previous exercises in this book provide your material for the array of achievements that you will choose for your CV.

CHOOSING THE RIGHT STYLE FOR YOUR CV

Fashions in CVs, as in most things, change over the years. The old-style 'tombstone' approach shown in Figure 9.1 is now out of favour. If your own CV uses this tired and hackneyed format, then you should change it, not because you are a slave to fashion but to improve your chances of a getting the job that is right for you.

THINGS TO AVOID IN YOUR CV

- Using a format that totally ignores your own *Prime Selling Points* and the *Key Competencies* required in the job that you are applying for.

- Adopting a template style that cannot be effectively amended and targeted to the specific purpose or job application.

- Wasting the top six inches of the front page by filling it with uninteresting background detail and hiding the most interesting information on the back page.

- Making your work experience difficult to read quickly.

- The first person – 'me', 'myself' and 'I' – should not be used. Saying 'I am a brilliant engineer,' can grate on the nerves, whereas 'An outstanding engineer with an excellent record,' is very acceptable.

- Putting potentially negative information on the front page, e.g. age. Relegate this kind of detail to the back page.

- Clutter the page with unnecessary headings such as Curriculum Vitae, Name, Address, etc.

- Giving boring and irrelevant details concerning educational modules.

- Salary details should not be included. If your current salary is less than the employer is willing to pay then you may harm your salary negotiating position. If it is more than the employer is offering then it raises doubts as to why you are applying for the job, and they might assume that you will not remain long in the position.

- Listing referees and addresses. On the few occasions when these are required in the initial stages of a job application, include them in the self-marketing letter that accompanies the CV.

Figure 9.1 A 'tombstone' CV

CURRICULUM VITAE

Personal details

Name:	Harvindr Singh Sandhu
Date of birth:	30–07–1966
Age:	37 years
Gender:	Male
Status:	Married

Address:	29 Lowbeam Avenue
	Rushington
	Notts
	NG4 6QZ

Telephone:	0115-642183
Mobile:	07747–622232
Email:	Harvsan@btnet.co.uk

Education

1993 – 1997	University of Trent, Nottingham
1985 – 1986	Lucknow University, Lucknow, India.
1981 – 1985	H.W. Inter College, Mohammdi, U.P., India.

Qualifications

Sep '96 – Jun '97	HND Computer Studies at University of Trent
Sep '94 – Jun '96	HNC Computer Studies (P/T) at University of Trent

Modules included:

Year 1	*Year 2*	*Year 3*
Introduction to IT	Advanced Systems	Analysis Maths for Computing
Program Design	Case & Quality Software	Data Com & Networks
Systems Analysis	Systems ('C') Programming	C++ Programming Industry
Software Engineering	Principles of Programming	Commercial Programming
MultiUser Databases	Data Structure	Algorithm Using C++

Sep '93 – Jun '94   BTEC Continuing Unit ('C' Programming)

Work experience

Apr '98 – June '03   **Analyst Programmer New Business Solutions, Nottingham**
Salary £23,000 pa
Our main business was to develop software for Apple Newton Notepad. Newton is a small computer without keyboard. A small plastic pen is used to write with. I was responsible for writing software using Visual Basic 3.0/ Access 2.0 to manage the host system, which communicates with Newton. While eight months at the company, I have also written a fully functional sales order processing system for a local company. We have also developed the entire system for Nottinghamshire Police.

Oct '96 – Apr '98   **Computor Tutor, Benitall Community Centre, Newark, Notts**
Fees: £8 per hour
Teaching Windows, Microsoft Office and C Programming to unemployed adults. Course was funded by Nottinghamshire County Coucil.

July '96 – Sep '96   **Freelance Programmer, Revolutionary Design, Lincoln**
Fees: £76 per day
Three-month contract working for Revolutionary. I was part of a small team working on a large project 'C' and Paradox for Windows.

Figure 9.1 continued

Oct '95 – Mar '96   Programmer, Abelard Systems Ltd
Salary: £16,000
My role while working with Abelard Systems covered most aspects of the Systems Development Life Cycle. On all projects I produced design for each program from a specification using a structure chart or data flow diagram. This then aided the coding for each program and also helped with later modifications. Finally I would test each program before returning it to the designer for system testing.

Sep '89 – Jun '92   Archaeological Surveyor, Archaeological Survey Team, Rushcliff
Salary: £9,000
Working as an Archaeological Surveyor gave me experience of working with a team of eight people on same project.

Mar '87 – June '89   Manager at Slick Sales Stores, Newark, Notts
Wage: £4.50 per hour
This involved managing a medium sized grocery store with three other part-time staff. Duties involved stock-taking, cash handling, book-keeping and staff management.

Other relevant information
Most of my computer experience has been based on IBM-compatibles using the MS-DOS operating system, programming in 'C' and 'C++'. I have also gained experience on other software packages including Microsoft Office, Windows 95 & 98, Foxpro 2, Adabas Natural, Borland C++ & Application Frameworks, Visual C++ and Paradox For Windows .

Hobbies and interests
I was Captain of Kabaddi Team (a contact sport) at college in India and now, as a member of Nottingham Sport Centre, I swim each week and play in the Squash League. Both sports are pursued in the interest of good health and fitness. I also enjoy minor car maintenance but only on my own car.

THE IMPORTANCE OF PRESENTATION

Using the second viewpoint, imagine yourself as a recruiter with a pile of CVs on your desk. Some of them have been folded and will not lie flat, others are on garishly coloured paper, some are handwritten. The untidy stack becomes daunting. Your eyes begin to glaze over after studying the first six or seven applications, searching through them for relevant facts. Little wonder that it is claimed that a CV initially gets only 20 or 30 seconds of the recruiter's attention.

Then you come across the example shown in Figure 9.2. It has been mailed, unfolded, in an A4 envelope and lies pristine and flat on the desk. It is printed on good quality paper.

Figure 9.2 A revised CV

Harvindr Singh Sandhu
29 Lowbeam Avenue, Rushington, Notts NG4 6QZ
Tel: 01662–642183

HND-qualified **Software Engineer** with excellent experience and proven skills in 'C++' programming language. A versatile and innovative professional who offers experience of a wide range of software packages, utilities and platforms. Commercially-aware, with the ability to provide an effective interface between customer requirements and computer-system solutions. An enthusiastic and self-motivated team member, with the determination and application to pursue projects to a successful conclusion.

Career History

1998 – 2003

New Business Solutions, Nottingham
ANALYST PROGRAMMER
Key role within a team developing specialist software for the miniature Apple Newton Notepad computer. Experience includes:
- Wrote and developed novel software solutions using Visual Basic 3.0 ∕ Access 2.0 to manage the host system, solving several complex interface problems and contributing to the successful product launch.
- Designed and implemented a fully functional sales order processing system for a local furniture company, meeting all customer specifications.
- Central involvement in developing the entire data storage and retrieval system for Nottinghamshire Police, using the Foxpro engine.

Oct '96 – Apr '98

Nottinghamshire County Council
COMPUTER TUTOR
Designed and presented a series of computer-training programmes for unemployed adults. Experience includes:
- Teaching basic and intermediate courses, covering Windows, Microsoft Office and C Programming.
- Dealing with people from all backgrounds and all levels of knowledge and ability, identifying individual training needs and helping each student to develop to the fullest potential.

July '96 – Sep '96

Revolutionary Design, Lincoln
FREELANCE PROGRAMMER
Key involvement in a small team working on a large project to produce a database on Windows 3.1 platform, gaining excellent experience in programming in C and Paradox languages.

Oct '95 – Mar '96

Abelard Systems Ltd.
PROGRAMMER
Received excellent training and experience in most aspects of the Systems Development Life Cycle.
- Produced the system design for each program from a specification using a structure chart or data flow diagram, aiding the coding for each program.
- Modifying programmes and liaising with the designer prior to final system testing.

Other experience, qualifications, and personal details

Previous experience

1989 – 1992

Archaeological Surveyor, Archaeological Survey Team, Rushcliff
Gained valuable experience in working within a collaborative team of eight people, agreeing objectives and jointly aiming to achieve them within a set timescale.

Figure 9.2 continued

1987 – 1989	**Manager at Slick Sales Stores, Newark, Notts** Working in a team of four, managing a grocery store, turnover £7,500 per week. Gained excellent training and experience in dealing with the general public, customer care, accurately handling cash, book-keeping and team leadership.
Qualifications	HND Computer Studies HNC Computer Studies BTEC Continuing Unit ('C' Programming) Cobol Programming Nottingham College of Further Education GCSE Mathematics, Physics Also Physics, Chemistry, English (University of Lucknow)
Other relevant information	Extensive computer experience based on IBM-Compatibles using the MS-DOS operating system, programming in 'C' and 'C++'. Also offers other valuable experience gained on software packages including Microsoft Office, Windows 95 & 98, Foxpro 2, Adabas Natural, Borland C++ & Application Frameworks, Visual C++ and Paradox For Windows .
Personal details	Date of birth: 30 July 1966 Gender: Male Marital status: Married Mobility: Full clean driving licence – own car Nationality: British
Leisure interests	Keep-fit Squash Swimming Maintaining own car

The chronological format in this example reuses the CV first used in Figure 9.1. The aim has been to demonstrate how even a difficult example can be transformed, while often retaining much of the original material. The new version shown in Figure 9.2 has been produced using the same information in the old tombstone style. The revised CV is a vast improvement on the original. It is stylish, easy-to-read, well planned, with the most relevant information boldly presented on the first page.

It offers the following advantages over the tombstone version:

- The layout has been improved.

- The main heading has been omitted – it is clear that this is a Curriculum Vitae anyway, so why state the obvious and waste a precious line of premium space.

- Superfluous subheadings – 'name', 'address' and so on – are no longer used.

- A personal profile has been added: it is an upbeat self-marketing statement designed initially to attract the recruiters' attention.

- All of the most important information regarding experience has been brought to the front page.

- Background facts and potential negatives have been consigned to the back page.

- The professional information has been reorganised into short, sharp bulletpoints. The tone has been changed to give a much more positive self-marketing image.

- Details of salary have been omitted.

- The most important qualification (HND) is mentioned in the profile, and the remainder of the rather boring list of qualifications has been relegated to page 2. It will be there to support the application once the recruiter is sufficiently interested by the opening points.

- The back page carries a 'header' stating the name and page number. This can be particularly important if you are faxing the CV to an employer; the second pages of different CVs can be easily mixed up.

- The layout showing qualifications on the back page has been drastically amended. Unnecessary or negative information has been omitted. The qualification itself is the important thing, not where it was obtained (unless the institution has particular significance), so these details have been left out. Dates of the qualifications are not listed either. It should be remembered that some qualifications can, quite literally, become outdated: an electronics degree in 1959 is almost irrelevant now, for example.

- Personal details are not key facts and are also on the back page. This is usually the best method, but there *could* be a different approach in this particular case. As the person's name is probably not familiar to non-Indian people, whether the person is male or female may not be readily apparent to most recruiters in the UK. Should they wait until the end of the CV before they know whether the applicant is a man or a woman? Gender should not be relevant and discrimination should not be facilitated or encouraged, and the argument has therefore been rejected here.

- Date of birth has been relocated to the foot of the second page. Note that the actual age is not stated: let the recruiters work it out for themselves. Stating an age dates a CV. It is probable that, subconsciously or otherwise, the recruiter has already worked out the age after reading the employment history, so it will come as no surprise to them. Some young people may think that their age is a positive advantage, but it is not always easy to know what preconceptions the recruiter may have. It is much better for the discerning employer to read your experience and attributes first.

- Details of referees have been omitted.

CONSIDERING OTHER FORMATS

The CV shown in Figure 9.1 presents some challenges in finding an effective format. This person is 37 years of age but he has not yet really established himself with any company for any length of time. It would not usually not be a good idea to litter the page with details of the year and months of any period of employment: stating 'July '96 – Sep '96' is not the preferred method of presentation; just '1996' is much better, particularly as this style can usefully conceal short periods between employment.

However, all cases are different. This person has moved between several short-term jobs in the same year, so in this instance it is necessary to show the months too. The point usefully illustrates that there can be no single 'right' way of organising a CV: you must make the best decision for your own particular circumstances, regardless of accepted convention.

There is another associated problem here: a stint of two or three months within a project can hardly be described as a key role. If it is (as in the case of very specialised consultancy work), then it should be described with strong achievement-led information, illustrating the expertise that can make a mark in such a very short timespan.

Once difficult presentational problems like this have been considered, there are many effective CV styles to choose from, but all conform to basic rules of sharp presentation and making best use of prime space on the page. Consider the differing types of layout used in Figures 9.3 and 9.4.

THE SINGLE-PAGE 'FLYER' CV

This is another example of a chronologically structured CV, but this time arranged on a single A4 page. It is often called a 'flyer' because in some ways it resembles an advertising leaflet, trimmed of all but the essentials. In actual fact, Figure 9.3 is something of a hybrid, because it still contains the detailed bullet selling points that are so important to the PSP system.

A one-page CV, if carefully designed, can be particularly effective. It can seem a little thin: 'It doesn't seem much to show for 20 years work!' is the kind of criticism that might be heard. This is a valid point, but skilful writing and editing can portray a very full and varied career on a single page. It is important that sufficient pertinent information is included, and there is literally no room for redundant words or uninteresting facts, so you must be very discriminating. Preparing a one-page 'flyer' such as this is an excellent exercise in trimming bloated text.

Figure 9.3 A one-page CV

PETER BRANFIELD

20 Grebe Close, Hemel Hempstead, Herts HP4 6YZ   Telephone: 01442 387777

Experienced LABORATORY ANALYST with an outstanding record achieved with a major international chemical manufacturer. Very reliable and flexible. Accustomed to working accurately and efficiently to GLP standards in a highly regulated industry.

QUALIFICATIONS

BSc in Applied Chemistry

HNC in Chemistry

CAREER HISTORY

1976 to 1997   Thomas Environmental Limited

(A Brandt & Masters joint venture company, turnover £30 million; formerly Johnson Chemicals and part of the IGA Group)

SENIOR LABORATORY ANALYST – QUALITY ASSURANCE

Key member of the Quality Assurance team responsible for testing all raw materials and finished products using standard methods, reporting and recording the results. Experience includes:

- Carrying out tests and analytical techniques using a variety of specified methods, including GLC and HPLC, IR and UV/Visible spectroscopy plus a variety of wet chemistry methods to check the compliance of raw materials, finished products and intermediates with agreed standards.
- Conforming with GLP standards in a laboratory working towards accreditation.
- Implementing approved sampling methods.
- Authorising the use of materials for processing.
- Calculating and checking quantities of raw materials for specified batch sizes in relation to analysed purity to ensure efficient use and compliance with product standards.
- Identifying areas of non-compliance and initiating corrective action to reduce production waste and minimise machine downtime.
- Investigating complaints and reporting findings to trace faults and initiate corrective action.
- Testing environmental and industrial waste samples prior to disposal, reporting the results.
- Calibration of equipment on a regular basis.
- Assisting in the ongoing assessment and amendment of test methods to improve accuracy and efficiency.
- Liaising with other key departments, including production services, manufacturing, product development, and maintenance engineering services.
- Maintaining high standards of operation and recording to ensure consistency, accuracy and safety in compliance with COSHH and Health & Safety legislation.
- Responding quickly and effectively to needs arising in the workplace.

PERSONAL DETAILS

Date of birth: 12 July 1960

Marital Status: Married, 3 children

Functional CV

A functional CV concentrates on the skills of the candidate rather than the jobs he or she has held. Sometimes such a CV hardly mentions the employment record, but expect some tough questioning at an interview if you adopt this approach (there is always the suspicion that you may have something to hide).

The functional or skills-based CV can be particularly useful if you are seeking to change your career path and your previous posts have little in common with the job you are seeking. This style can also be useful when you want to emphasise your skills rather than your record, even if you are staying within the same industry, especially if you are trying to jump to a higher level.

The example shown in Figure 9.4 is a two-page skills-based CV. Again, you will see that there is some intentional overlapping of CV types. It makes a concession to the chronological format by giving details of the current employment role, but then immediately goes on to give a list of differing skills. It makes no mention of previous employment, although a short summary could be added if expedient: dates, job title and name of employer, for example.

This format can be useful in a variety of situations, and particularly if you are applying for another position within the same company (or even if you are having to reapply for your current position, as sometimes happens).

MAKING DECISIONS ABOUT YOUR CV

This chapter has discussed the various aspects of an effective CV. The aim has been to provoke thoughts regarding a suitable layout for your own documents. Remember, there are no 'right' or 'wrong' ways, merely more or less effective ones. Rather than worry about what the latest fashion or convention is, consider what type of format is best for you and the specific job application.

Figure 9.4 Two-page skills-based CV

Graham Till

Fishery Wharf
Fishery Road
Boxmoor
Hemel Hempstead
HP1 1NA

Telephone: 01442 215020
Mobile: 07747 025242
geeveetee@geeveetee.plus.com

> **Senior Manager and Career Management professional** with an outstanding track record. A skilled coach and presenter offering proven consulting and project management skills with the ability to help clients at all corporate levels. Has an in-depth knowledge of the outplacement industry with a wide network throughout the UK. Strong reputation in establishing and maintaining long-term business partnerships with major sponsors on behalf of the Consultancy. Very innovative and resourceful motivator with a reputation for achieving results.

SKILLS AND ACHIEVEMENTS

- Successfully led the National Division of a PLC, with personal responsibility for business development and P&L producing £1.5 million turnover p.a. with a net profit of £600,000. Took a negative start-up point and personally developed the Division to a viable and profitable unit within the first six months.

- Exceptional Outplacement Project Management skills with strong record in successfully establishing, staffing and coordinating outplacement assignments at locations throughout the UK. An ability to plan and manage complex tasks within exacting budgets.

- In-depth knowledge and wide network of freelance associates within the outplacement consultancy sector.

- Strong knowledge and particular expertise in operating effectively and appropriately in trade union organised workplaces.

- Outplacement consultant with a wealth of experience in providing face to face support for clients at all corporate levels.

- Outstanding team leadership skills, with the ability to build and develop strong, relevant teams.

- Strong literary skills – published author with proven ability in producing effective proposals.

- Experienced trainer and presenter of workshops. Excellent presentation skills, either using Microsoft Powerpoint or traditional methods. Able to relate effectively with people at all corporate levels.

MAIN QUALIFICATION

MA in Industrial Relations and HR Management   University of Keele

CAREER MANAGEMENT HISTORY

Globeskills Limited	Chairman	2003 to date
Fairplace Consulting plc	Director – National HR Services	1995 – 2002
Coutts Career Consultants	Freelance Project Manager	1990 – 1995

Figure 9.4 continued

Graham Till 2/2

CAREER HISTORY

Fairplace Consulting plc   1995 to 2002
Director – National HR Services

Successfully led the Division, producing £1.5 million turnover p.a. with a net profit of £600,000

- Took a negative start-up point and personally developed the Division to a viable and profitable unit within the first six months.

- Demonstrated excellent entrepreneurial skills, designing and developing the company's successful group outplacement concept and delivery model.

- Recruited and developed a wide network of associate outplacement consultants throughout the UK, successfully delivering diverse on-site projects within the Company model.

- Business development, building and maintaining excellent client relationships with an emphasis on repeat business.

- Strong budgetary control, running the operation with a small, lean team and exceptionally low overheads.

- Exceptional team leader with hands-on management ability, including service delivery and project management.

Project Manager and Consultant
Successfully managed many large-scale on-site projects, leading outplacement teams comprised of consultants, trainers and job search staff.

Extensive experience in providing outplacement coaching to clients from a diverse range of sectors.

Sponsors include:

- BOC – Guildford

- Aventis CropScience (formerly AgrEvo)

- Booker Wholesale (several projects across the UK)

- Jewsons, Huddersfield and Newbury

- Amoco, London

- Nurdin & Peacock

- Horticultural Research Institute (HRI)

Coutts Career Consultants   1990 to 1995
Freelance Project Manager and Outplacement Consultant

British Rail Engineering Ltd (latterly BREL)   1979 to 1990
Employee Relations

OTHER INFORMATION

Published author, including *How to Get Your Next Job* and numerous articles.

In the next chapter, there is a step-by-step guide to writing an effective CV, using the material that you have already gathered from the previous exercises.

1. Your CV is self-marketing literature. It advertises your product: the package of skills, experience and ability that you have especially assembled for a specific job application.

2. The ability to produce effective and winning CVs is probably the most important part of your job-getting system. The purpose of your CV is *not* solely to generate an interview. It is also:

    – a self analysis and marketing tool;

    – a potential agenda for your subsequent interview;

    – a script for interviews;

    – a defence against potentially negative points.

3. First impressions are overwhelmingly important. The presentation must be first class with an appealing visual layout. White space is as important as black; use wide margins with consistent spacing. Use top quality white or ivory paper.

4. Decide whether to use a chronological or a functional CV format. As a general rule, use the 'functional' style which lists your skills if you are changing your career path; if continuing in your present kind of job, use the chronological CV and describe your experience within the structure of a conventional career history.

5. When listing your employment record, start with your present/most recent job and work backwards. Recruiters are interested in what you are now rather than what you were 20 years ago.

6. Make sure that your *Prime Selling Points* for the job are boldly stated in the main impact area of the CV, i.e. in the profile and also as leading bullet points in the top six inches of the first page.

7. Be positive and use plenty of dynamic words and phrases, e.g. enhanced, designed and implemented, organised, drove the project to a successful conclusion, and so on.

8. Clearly state your achievements, and quantify them with some indication of scale.

9. Use short, interesting bullet points to describe each skill or aspect of your experience. Aim for sharply-drawn pen pictures of no more than two sentences.

10. Assume that the reader does not know your industry and write in plain, easy to understand terms. However, if you are applying for a job within your specialist field, it is permissible to use some industry-specific jargon whereby fellow professionals will recognise you as one of their own.

Some don'ts

11. Don't use the first person 'I' – it is irritating, unprofessional and unnecessarily litters the page.

12. Don't be too modest.

13. Don't overestimate the perceptiveness of recruiters or expect them to read between the lines.

14. Don't list your referees.

15. Don't give your salary details.

16. Don't state your reasons for leaving a company.

Remember, a recruiter will see hundreds of different CV styles, ranging from the tombstone versions to triple-folded brochures and all manner of gimmicks. Avoid the temptation to use gimmickry: it is a poor statement to make about yourself and devalues your candidature for any job.

Be very critical of your own document, without prejudice caused by other factors: do not use a poor CV just because your son/daughter/spouse/best friend lovingly produced it for you, or because you feel that you have a special sense of pride and 'ownership' of the document. Take a long hard look in the light of information contained here and be prepared to drastically revise and reformat the material. Only the best is good enough for you!

Chapter 10
Writing a winning CV

USE THIS CHAPTER TO PRODUCE YOUR OWN **CV**

Having considered the various issues of a CV, you should now begin to actually write your main document: this will form the basis of most subsequent amendments to produce individually targeted documents for each specific job application.

You will need:

■ reference material compiled from the exercises in this book.

■ a quantity of A4 100 g/m^2 white or cream paper.

■ a means of word processing and printing (or at least typing) your finished document.

A QUESTION OF STYLE

For the purposes here, and to get the maximum value with the least complexity, three CV styles are used: chronological, functional, and a hybrid between the two.

Chronological

This style delivers bulleted selling points organised within a framework of your employment history, starting with your current/most recent job and working backwards. It is very effective if you have a long history within one company or a background that features the same kind of work and the job you are seeking is in a similar field using the same skills. It is also a good style for showing how and where skills were acquired and demonstrating career progression.

Functional

A CV that concentrates upon functions rather than employment history is useful if you are seeking a job which is rather different from those you have done in the past. It will highlight transferable and relevant skills drawn from your previous jobs.

This format offers a good way of dealing with 'difficult' employment history features: an inconsistent or varied career history, uneven career progression with backward steps, long periods of unemployment or even imprisonment.

Hybrid

A cross between the two main styles has emerged in recent years. It is nearer to the functional type as the emphasis is upon key skills. However, the employment history is also shown, usually in a supporting role, with a brief description and some important bulleted selling points for each job. It is necessarily less detailed than the chronological style, however.

The hybrid format is particularly useful when the recruiter is probably very familiar with the content of your previous jobs. It also enables the candidate to show career and skills progression while highlighting *Prime Selling Points*. This is very effective when done well, as it contains both a skills list *and* a roll of achievements structured as a chronological career history. However, it is not an easy format to work with and requires very focused editing to ensure that only key material is used in the limited space that is available.

CHOOSING THE STYLE THAT IS RIGHT FOR YOU

You can either decide from the outset which of the three main styles is best suited for your purposes, or you can take a more gradual approach, starting with a chronological format and changing if necessary.

Some people make an objective judgement about which format to use and simply begin to write their CV. This is reasonable enough because the first test is in the writing: as the work progresses it is frequently found that another style is preferable for the particular needs.

> It is a good idea to keep a long 'library resource' version of a CV. This will be an exhaustive list of skills and achievements – more than will be used in any single job application – listed within the chosen CV structure. It is then only necessary to 'cut and paste' the best material for each particular occasion to produce a very effective targeted self-marketing document.

The recommended approach is to begin with a chronological format as this will gather most of the relevant material together in a simple and logical structure. The work will soon show whether this version is suitable for your needs. It is easy to rework the draft if another format is preferred. Even if you decide to change styles, this groundwork will not be wasted, particularly if using a word processor that can save and reorganise the selling points to best advantage. Indeed, in preparing a first-draft chronological CV, you will probably amass far more material that can be used in any single CV. Do not throw any of it away.

WHICH FONT?

The font that you use is largely a matter of personal preference. It is a good idea to match the print style to your own personality and also for the image of the job: choose between the more traditional and staid fonts, e.g. Times Roman, or the modern and clean-cut sans serif types, such as Arial. There seems little point in using the flexibility of a word processor to mimic a typewriter with the Courier font:

Times New Roman 12 pt.

Times New Roman 10 pt.

Arial 12 pt

Arial 10 pt

Courier 12 pt

There are no hard and fast rules, but it is probably a good idea to use Times Roman for senior and managerial posts or for 'pillar of society' type roles. The modern electronic 'sunrise' industries seem to particularly like the sharp, uncomplicated modern fonts. However, there is no evidence to support these views. On the other hand, it is important to avoid unconventional typefaces: they might get your application noticed but usually at the expense of credibility.

Importantly, make sure that the print is large enough to read easily. Indeed, the size of print can influence the style of font that you choose. If it is necessary to go down to 10 point, use a sans serif such as Arial, which keeps a nice clean and legible appearance at smaller sizes; Time Roman can be too small and fiddly at this size. On the other hand, a larger size arguably gives Arial a somewhat vulgar appearance.

Do not change fonts in the document; it is an irritatingly bad practice that declares a lack of knowledge in presentation. It is, however, permissible to use differing sizes and emboldened or italicised characters of the same font to emphasise headings and so on. There is also a question of whether to use upper or lower case letters for headings, and of what size type they should be.

Figure 10.1 outlines a smart, modern presentation that looks fresh and up to date. This style looks particularly attractive in Arial 10 point font when producing a single-page CV. Figure 10.2 outlines a more sober presentation using the Times New Roman typeface, centred headings and a traditional style.

Figure 10.1 Stylesheet

Font: Arial

Name Heading, Left Justified, Title Case, 16 point

Address and telephone number, left justified, 10 or 12 point plain text.

Profile (if used): regular 12 point text, justified left with **key words in bold.**

Main Headings: Centred, Title Case, bold 14 point

Sub Headings: Left Justified, Title Case, Bold 12 Point

Ordinary text: 10 or 12 point, justified left.

Choose between a right or left justification for dates of Employment History

Sparingly used lines are often effective in this format.

Figure 10.2 Stylesheet

Font: Times New Roman

NAME: CENTRED, UPPER CASE 16 POINT
Address and Telephone Number: 10–12 point plain text, centred

Profile, if used, in 12 point text, **left justified**, whtin a fine-line box, using **emboldened highlights** for emphasis of key relevant information

MAIN HEADINGS: CENTRED, UPPER CASE BOLD 14 POINT

Subheadings: Centred, Title Case, Bold 12 Point

Ordinary text: 10 or 12 point Times New Roman, left justified

Choose between a right or left justification for dates of employment history

The styles shown in the two examples are for guidance rather than slavish adherence. Some features of each can be combined: the case and page justification of headings, for example. However, you should be consistent in the use of particular style throughout the whole document.

If in any doubt, use the style demonstrated in the step-by-step word processor guide at the end of this chapter. This will always produce a smart and effective document.

Your CV structure

Assuming that you have been doing the exercises in this book, most of the hard work for your CV has already been completed. Either take an A4 pad and pencil or work directly on a PC with a word processor and follow the steps shown below to begin constructing your 'library resource' chronological CV.

Try to write this as you intend it to appear in the final version of the CV, especially if you are going to hand this to someone else for typing. The sheets you produce here will form your draft copy.

1   Begin by writing your name and address and contact details.

Set out your name and address as follows:

William J Merrill

22 The Bards' Cottages

Cannon Street

Cookham

Berkshire

SL7 6NN

Telephone: 01628 446778

Mobile: 07743 642918

E-mail: bill.merrill@virgin.net

It is worth noting the things that are intentionally omitted in this opening title section:

- the superfluous 'Curriculum Vitae' heading is absent;
- descriptive subheadings – 'Name', 'Address' and so on – are dispensed with;
- commas and full stops are not used, in keeping with the modern business style and providing a cleaner style of presentation.

A more debatable point is whether to list your work telephone number. Some recruiters frown on the notion that you are the sort of person who uses company time and resources to obtain another job: 'If this person does that to the current employer, then he or she is also likely to do it to us, too.' Other recruiters are less pernickety about such concerns and employment agencies don't care at all. This is a judgement that you must make for yourself but it is recommended that you eliminate any potentially negative features, especially in this most prominent part of your CV.

> When choosing an e-mail address, it is worth remembering that frivolous attempts at humour or dubious innuendo can look rather pathetic on CVs or other job-getting documents. For example, 'silly.billy' or 'partygirl' could seriously damage your chances of being taken seriously.

If working with a word processor, you can save considerable time and effort by using the cut and paste function.

The following step-by-step guide will assist. Lay this title sheet aside for the time being.

2 **List your career history in the manner that it will be shown on your CV, taking your employment record and job record sheets compiled in Chapter 8 (Figures 8.1 and 8.2) as a starting point.**

Starting with your current or most recent job, transcribe the details in the following manner: dates, name of employer, town/city and county, job title, summary description of the job. At this stage include all of the information on your individual job record. You can start to sort this material by ranking the various points in a rough order of importance. Make sure that you include at least one bullet selling point for each general competency.

Using a new page for each separate job, repeat this transcription process until you have reorganised the material contained in your job record sheets (see the example shown in Figure 10.3).

Starting with the most recent job, copy the starting and finishing dates of this period of employment (if still in the job, simply write '– to date').

1. Using the job record, transcribe the summary of purpose relating to that job.

2. Now list the most important bullet points for each job, including general competency points.

3. Repeat for all of your previous jobs, using a separate sheet of paper for each one. However, the further back in your working life, the less you need to give a lot of detail, and it is reasonable to reduce the number of bullet points.

Figure 10.3 Job record sheet

1987 – to date   **Name of employer**
Optima Health Co., Guildford
PA/Secretary

Responsible for providing full secretarial and administrative support to two Production Services Executives and the Production Services Manager of a pharmaceutical company (turnover £23 million p.a.).

Main points
- Word processing of all correspondence, reports and presentations, using Microsoft Word and Powerpoint software.
- Preparing a key monthly reconciliation report, using an Excel spreadsheet, to demonstrate traceability of hydrocarbon oils for Customs & Excise purposes.
- Setting up spreadsheets and entering data.
- Answering general enquiries, organising travel, office administration, daily updating the 'in-house' computerised stock control system, maintaining records of the department, staff holidays and sickness.
- Managing the office in the absence of the Manager.

Achievements
- Ability and effort recognised with promotion after commencing as a typist.
- Reorganised the reporting systems for collating information used by HM Customs & Excise, using Excel spreadsheets.

If you have received payment in lieu of notice and are still within the contractual period of a job, you can still legitimately show the dates of employment as continuing. For example, if you commenced a job in 1992 and left it in February 2003, but the employer gave you wages until May, you can write '1992 to date' up to May even though you no longer attend the company premises or do the job.

When this has been completed, file the sheets in reverse order, i.e. your current or most recent job should be uppermost.

3   Detail relevant education, qualifications and vocational training

You must now produce a listing of your qualifications and training, starting with the most important and/or senior qualification.

As a general point, it is tempting to go into great detail over things that mean a lot to you, even if it is of little interest to the recruiter. For example, many people give every last detail of their university degree course, listing every module, the full methodology and so on. This is both unnecessary and counter productive in that it is boring and wastes valuable space. It is much better to simply write: 'BSc in Mathematics – University of Keele'.

Employers want details of your qualifications rather than the place of learning, but it is usual to include the university name when listing degrees. It is certainly best to omit the names of schools and colleges unless they have specific relevance to your application (some establishments are particularly prestigious, for example). Educational reform in the UK over the past few years has resulted in many schools merging, changing names or closing. The name of a school which nobody other than ex-pupils has ever head of will add little value to the CV. Few employers ever check this information anyway.

The same applies to vocational studies and qualifications: details of the course and qualification will usually suffice.

Be concise and brief when detailing qualifications:

City & Guilds, Parts 1, 2 & 3, in Bricklaying (with Credit)

not:

Luton Polytechnic	*City & Guilds Part 1 (PASS) Bricklaying*
Luton Polytechnic	*City & Guilds Part 2 (CREDIT) Bricklaying*
Luton Polytechnic	*City & Guilds Part 3 (PASS) Bricklaying*

Do not list all the various modules and pass marks of a course.

The following is an example of a list of qualifications and training

BSc in Applied Chemistry
HNC in Chemistry

3 'A' levels: Maths, Physics and Chemistry
6 'O' levels

In-house training courses include:
Supervisory Management
Interaction Management, Parts 1 and 2
COSHH Awareness
COSHH Workshop
Fire Extinguisher Training

There may be a case for listing your main qualification on the front page of the CV, but this decision can be made later.

4   List any professional memberships

Once the Qualifications and training section is completed, using the same sheet of paper, detail any memberships of professional bodies, taking care to list them correctly. (Professional institutes are notoriously sensitive to inaccurately quoted titles.) The following is a typical example:

'Chartered Member of the Institute of Mechanical Engineers'

Again, you may feel it appropriate to promote this section to the front page if it is particularly important in any given job application.

5   List your personal details

If there is room, continue on the same sheet of paper so that your qualifications, training, memberships and personal details are readily to hand.

List the following details in the manner as shown:

Date of birth:	19 February 1966
Marital status:	Married, 2 children
Mobility:	Full clean driving licence, own car.

Many people choose to omit their age from a CV. Why? The omission could be taken to indicate a personal preoccupation about ageing.

Always show that you have a driving licence and car, even if driving has nothing to do with the job for which you are applying. It shows that you are able to get there without problems. One company with premises situated at an isolated spot on the Yorkshire moors is reluctant to employ females in particular unless they have their own transport, not least because of the safety of their employees. If you have penalty points on your licence, simply write 'Full driving licence…' Foreign nationals may wish to put 'Full *UK* driving licence'. These are the kinds of points that make all the difference and that you need to consider.

Whether or not you mention children is, again, a matter of personal judgement. Unfortunately, even in this supposed world of equal opportunities, discrimination on the grounds of gender is still rife. Bluntly, a man with children can signal *stability*, while a woman with children can be interpreted as *liability*. It is not clear why this should be so when more and more couples share child-raising responsibilities, but old views die hard. It perhaps does not pay to encourage it or pander to it.

However, such discrimination can sometimes lose you an otherwise good interview opportunity. Ignore the old saw that a company that exercises such discrimination is not worth working for because it is more than likely nothing to do with the company, but the personality defect of a bigoted recruiter whom you may never see again after being employed. The best advice, as always, is to remove any potential negative features from your CV: if in doubt, leave it out.

6   Add your leisure interests

The usefulness of including seemingly irrelevant leisure pursuits has often been questioned. Recruiters do seem to like them, however, arguing that they provide some insight into a 'more rounded' person. They can certainly provide ice-breakers at an interview. So, on balance, it is best to include them.

Not 'hobbies', it will be noted, but 'Leisure Interests'. This can usefully include things such as work as a school governor, or charity fund-raising, both of which say positive things about your ability and character. One single line can suffice:

Cricket, Home maintenance and Backgammon

However, much better would be:

Cricket – player in local league side and treasurer of Club
Home maintenance
Backgammon – regular tournament player

Also, of course, this section can be used to highlight certain skills and attributes that may not be apparent from other parts of the CV. The effectiveness of any given leisure interest cannot always be gauged in advance: one person who listed 'restoring classic cars' as a leisure activity was selected for interview purely because of this fact, and it transpired that the job concerned matching specialist chrome plating for the parts of vintage cars.

Be careful not to list so many activities that it seems that you rarely have time for work. For the same reason this also applies to showing low golf handicaps, for example. Three or four interests will suffice, and the best advice is to include a balanced selection: a cerebral pursuit (e.g. chess or geneology); a physical activity (e.g. sport, keep-fit or sailing); a 'doing' thing (e.g. gardening or home maintenance); a community-oriented activity (e.g. running a youth club).

As a golden rule, steer clear of religion, politics or blood sports when listing personal interests! There is no point in unnecessarily alienating someone with strongly opposing views.

Some advise omitting from your list any sports that involve violence – boxing, martial arts and so on. Quite apart from any philosophical objections, some recruiters are deterred by the prospect of employing people who are liable to be absent due to injury as a result of dangerous pursuits. On the other hand, others would argue that such activities demonstrate self-control, dedication and self-reliance. If you do follow leisure pursuits such as these, think about whether you should include them on the CV.

The inclusion of leisure interests can be useful in deflecting attention from unwelcome personal details such as age: the first and last parts of a document are usually the things that most people remember. Using this reasoning, it might be asked why this slot is not used for more important information but it has been tried and, for some reason, it does not work.

When this page has been completed, it should contain the following detailed sections:

▧ Qualifications, training and education

▧ Professional memberships (optional)

▧ Personal details

▧ Leisure interests.

File this page at the rear of your CV folder, behind the sheets that make up your career history.

7   Finally, write a personal profile

The short pen picture that both introduces and summarises your CV is probably the hardest part to write. It is very important, because it is your banner headline, and recruiters seeking a 'short read' may make an initial paper-sift using this kind of information.

It is particularly difficult to write a personal profile for yourself because it requires a skill in self-promotion that few of us naturally possess. It is easier to compose a good opening paragraph for a friend. You may therefore wish to get someone to help you with this part of the CV.

In any event, it may need several attempts before you get a good working draft. This will inevitably be changed several times in the future because the profile lends itself to customising to highlight experience and skills that are relevant to the specific job application.

A good profile should be limited to the following:

▧ a reference to essential or much sought-after qualifications;

▧ a term to describe what you do: buyer, sales manager, administrative worker, etc.;

▧ a short summary of your *Prime Selling Points*.

Unsupported, self-congratulatory and boastful terms like 'dynamic' and 'self-motivated' tend to be empty and meaningless. In fact they have devalued personal profiles to the point where some people totally ignore them. The reasoning here, based on extensive experience, is that a well-written and targeted profile still plays a significant part in a successful job-getting CV. This will only be a few lines and certainly no more than a single paragraph.

The following examples give a reasonable idea of the type of thing that you need:

Sales Manager with a very successful record, extensive experience and high-level contacts in the UK automobile industry. Offers the proven ability to lead teams to generate exceptional sales revenue, achieving a gross sales turnover of £8 million in 1998 (an increase of 120 per cent on the previous year).

or:

An efficient Secretary and PA, with valuable experience achieved supporting the senior executive of a major multinational organisation. Record demonstrates excellent organisational and administrative skills, with the ability to work on own initiative and under pressure. Accustomed to maintaining confidentiality in a commercially-sensitive working environment.

or:

Chartered Engineer with an outstanding record and proven ability in the design and installation of viable Air Separation Units at sites throughout the world.

First or second person are not generally favoured: the words 'me', 'myself' and 'I' are not used in any of the above examples, and neither is there any reference to 'she' or 'he'. A more abstract approach is preferred instead.

When you are reasonably satisfied with an initial form of words for your personal profile, transcribe the paragraph onto the title page beneath your name and address.

The major groundwork for your library resource CV has now been completed. You should now have the following sheets in your folder, filed in the order as shown:

- *Title sheet* — Detailing name, address, telephone numbers
  Personal profile
- *Job record sheets* — A separate job record sheet for each of your previous jobs
- *Personal details* — Qualifications, education and training
  Leisure interests

The next step is to reproduce this information in a usable chronological format. After entering the name, address and so on, simply transcribe each separate job in your career history, including every separate bullet point. The example shown in Figure 10.4 should be used as a style template.

Do not worry at this stage if there are too many bullet points and too much material to fit on the pages. This is your main library resource document. It will be ruthlessly edited when you produce CVs for actual job applications. However, it would be a shame not to see the fruits of your labours at this point, and it will also be useful to have a CV for general use.

Figure 10.4 Career history

John Collins
33 Newfoundland Way
Berkhamsted
Hertfordshire
HP4 7LZ

Tel. 01422 556789
E-mail:jcollins@patrol.i-way.co.uk

Experienced **Software Programmer** with an extensive and up-to-date knowledge of C++ and Cobol. Programming and software development skills are built upon a sound base of process and mechanical engineering skills and qualifications. A proactive team member with a record of success in providing innovative software solutions to problems.

Career History

1995 to date   **Tom Rowlinson and Associates, Hemel Hempstead**
(1997 to date)   **SENIOR SOFTWARE ENGINEER**
Key role in writing code and developing new commercial software to resolve problems raised by Y2k+ (Year 2000) compliance requirements. Experience and achievements include:
- Wrote and developed novel software solutions using Cobol to create a diagnostic tool to identify potential problems with Y2k+.
- Liaised with other programmers within the team, integrating various software components to create a fully integrated package for commercial sale.
- Trained and motivated junior programmers, identifying their training needs and providing intensive personal coaching.
- Designed and implemented a fully functional sales order processing system for a local furniture company, communicating with the customer at all management and functional levels, meeting all specifications.

(1995 to 1997)   **PROGRAMMER**
- Working within a team, with central involvement in developing the entire data storage and retrieval system for Nottinghamshire Police, using the Foxpro engine.
- Received comprehensive training in structured programming of both customised and new proprietary applications using C++ and Cobol. Also experienced in SQL language.

1996 to 1998   **Nottinghamshire County Council**
COMPUTER TUTOR
Responsible for the design and presentation of a series of computer-training programmes for unemployed adults. Experience includes:
- Teaching basic and intermediate courses, covering Windows, Microsoft Office and C Programming

Figure 10.4 continued

John Collins   Page 2/2

| 1994 to 1996 | **Boroughs Engineering Processes, Bracknell** |

1994 to 1996   **Boroughs Engineering Processes, Bracknell**
GRADUATE ENGINEERING TRAINEE
Received a thorough grounding in all aspects of process engineering, successfully completing a structured training programme involving work in all aspects of the business. Experience includes:
- Auditing and identifying customer requirements, involving extensive liaison with staff at all corporate levels.
- Using Hysem computerised engineering simulation software to analyse structural designs.

(1995)
- Gained Trainee of the Year Award in competition with over 100 other staff world-wide

Education, qualifications and training

BSc in Mechanical Engineering – University of Bath

HND Computer Studies

HNC Computer Studies

BTEC Continuing Unit ('C' Programming)

A Levels: Mathematics, English and Physics

GCSE Mathematics, English, Physics, Chemistry, Biology

Training courses include:

Cobol Programming

C++ for Commercial Programmers

Finance for Non-Financial Managers

Personal details

Date of birth	26 February 1969
Status	Married, 2 children
Mobility	Full clean driving licence
	Non-smoker

Leisure interests

Hockey (county player), cricket, building customised cars, writing, travel.

So cut out some of the less important bullet selling points until the text fits onto the page. Try not to leave 'widows and orphans': bullet points that start on one page and finish on another. In fact, it is best to try to keep periods of employment together on a page.

Make sure that your name and the page number is inserted at the top of page 2. If there is enough room, separate different sections with a couple of line spaces.

Be prepared to examine your work critically and revise the CV until you are satisfied.

Chapter 11

Writing self-marketing letters

THIS CHAPTER IS DEVOTED TO THE PRINCIPLES OF WRITING EFFECTIVE SELF MARKETING LETTERS.

Contacting potential employers is an important part of any job-getting campaign. First impressions do count, so it is necessary that effective techniques are used from the outset. Even a well-crafted and targeted CV is not enough on its own. It requires an equally effective self-marketing letter to accompany it. Indeed, it can be argued that your self-marketing letter is initially more important than the CV it introduces. A poor covering letter will ruin the impact of the best CV. This chapter is therefore devoted to the principles of writing effective self-marketing letters.

In the Globeskills job-getting system, there are several different purposes for such letters but all types are produced using the same formula. This method has proven very effective in competitive job markets and it produces letters that are both easy to write and read. You can achieve a professional, business-like approach with every letter you write if you follow the recommendations, including those concerning punctuation, formatting and content. However, if you wish to use a different style of presentation, the advice regarding content remains pertinent.

TYPES OF SELF-MARKETING LETTER

There are a number of purposes for self marketing letters:

- to accompany and introduce your CV in response to a job advert;

- to accompany and introduce an application form and your CV;

- to accompany your skills and career résumé sheet (or your full CV, if you choose to send it) to a recruitment agency;

- as a direct speculative approach to an employer;

- to solicit information and accompany your CV to a personal networking contact.

THE ESSENTIALS

Your address and telephone number

Many employers prefer to use the telephone or, increasingly, e-mail messages rather than letters to make contact with applicants. Always be sure to include your full address, postcode, telephone number(s) and, if appropriate, your e-mail address.

All of these details should be placed on the right hand of the page. It should not be centred as if on a company letterhead; it is not good practice and can make an unwitting, negative statement about a lack of knowledge or commitment to convention.

Date

In the standard format recommended here, the date should be expressed in full but without punctuation: 28 August 200X. It is usually placed on the left-hand side of the page, above the recipient's name and address.

Recipient's details

It is much better to address your letter to a named manager rather than generally to the company, or to the Personnel Department. Always use the manager's name, rather than 'Dear Sir or Madam'. Using the name of the appropriate manager personalises your approach, and it also enables you to mark the envelope 'Private and Confidential', with a reasonable expectation that it will arrive on the manager's desk unopened.

> If making a direct approach, always address your letter to the most senior and relevant line manager. Do not address it to the personnel manager. The job of personnel managers is to stop you getting a job if the budgeted departmental staffing quota is already full; your enquiry is likely to end in the bin without any relevant manager ever seeing it.

If responding to an advertisement, most of the required details are usually supplied. You should certainly always conform with the instructions given. However, too many advertisements merely give the manager's name with no indication of title or job title: 'Reply with full CV to Angela Smith…'

You should make sure that you use the manager's preferred salutation (Mr, Mrs, Dr, Miss or Ms), and also his or her correct job title. Other essentials are the full company name, address and postcode. Telephone the company to check any of these details.

Salutation

If writing to an employer, use the formal method of address – 'Dear Mrs Smith' – even if the manager's first name is supplied in the job advertisement. On the hand, if replying to an employment agency, you may wish to use the person's first name because that is acceptable in the industry; if you do, as a courtesy, always make sure that you sign off with your own first and last names rather than initials. Again, to achieve a crisp and clean presentation, punctuation is omitted.

Heading

If writing in response to an advertisement or forwarding an application form you should use a heading to make it clear which job you are applying for *and quote any reference numbers*. The heading should be in emboldened text and, in the format recommended here, it is justified to the left-hand side of the page.

You could also use a brief descriptive heading when writing a speculative letter, but be careful not to be over-specific and risk being ignored for a vacancy that might not fit your description.

Format

A three-paragraph, bullet-pointed format is both easy to write and easy to read. More importantly, it has been proven to be very effective in getting the message across neatly and quickly. The three components of this sharp self-marketing letter are:

1. *'The Tempter'* paragraph, introducing yourself, stating why you are writing, and opening with a statement that says what you can do for the employer instead of what the employer can do for you. This paragraph also introduces your CV and, as the name implies, it should make the recruiter want to read on.

2. *Your Prime Selling Points*: no more than five bullet points – short statements that each illustrate how you match the *Key Competencies Required* of the job.

3. *'Action'* paragraph. This concluding paragraph is used to state what you intend to do to follow up the letter, and what you would like to happen next. Candidates for senior roles usually ask for a meeting rather than an interview.

This formula ensures that all relevant information is included and that your best selling points are very clearly proclaimed. Yet it occupies a single A4 page and can be read in less than 30 seconds. Although this is a very tight format, there is still room to include supporting statements and information.

The Tempter paragraph stakes your claim to be an excellent candidate for the job. The bulleted *Prime Selling Points* that follow should expand upon that statement and demonstrate just why you should be selected for interview.

Signing off

Always conclude your letter with 'Yours sincerely' when writing to a named person (otherwise, sign off with 'Yours faithfully'). Allow a space of six carriage returns for your signature and then add your first and last names. In the format used here, both the sign-off and your name should be left-justified.

THINGS TO AVOID

By placing yourself in the second and third viewpoint positions and viewing the letter from a manager's perspective, you will understand that if faced with 100 or more letters of application, you would initially be seeking 'deselectors' to get the list down to manageable proportions. It is therefore apparent that the content of your letter should make it as difficult as possible to reject your application at this stage so it is important to avoid any potential negatives.

Weaknesses

It is not your responsibility to highlight any deficiencies in your candidacy for any job. You are making a job application, not going to a confessional! In the words of the song, accentuate the positive, and eliminate the negative.

Do not use phrases like, 'Although I have no experience in this field…' or 'Although I am 54 years of age…' Neither should you mention that you do not have a particular qualification that is mentioned in the advertisement.

Waffle

A chatty and rambling approach will not win friends in a busy recruiter's office. Irrelevant detail is counterproductive.

Silliness

In the search for impact many people unwisely adopt an aggressive sales pitch or attempted humour. One candidate, for example, opened his letter with 'Congratulations, you have the opportunity to employ the best Production Supervisor in the soft drinks industry.' Another wrote, 'Grease and Lightning are my middle names.' This kind of gimmick rarely, if ever, works.

Empty flattery

Sycophantic and ingratiating comments can spoil job applications. Managers do not want to constantly read how wonderful their employer is. It is pointless stating that you admire the company and have heard that it is a good outfit to work for. The recruiter assumes that you want to work for the company simply because you have applied for the job!

Why you are in the job market

It is neither appropriate nor necessary to state your reasons for seeking a new job. That is not to say why you should not give positive reasons for applying for this particular vacancy (wholly different to empty flattery). Of course, this is a question that is likely to be asked at some stage, but the purpose of the self-marketing letter is to get you to an interview where the matter can be handled face to face.

THINGS TO INCLUDE

The Tempter paragraph should include a sentence that states where you saw the advertisement. Use italics for the name of publications, and show the date in closed brackets: *Daily Telegraph* (30 July). This demonstrates attention to detail and also provides feedback on the effectiveness of a company's advertising media.

Demonstrate that you have done your homework on the company: refer to newspaper articles or the job specification and so on. These can be included as single sentence comments: 'I read with interest the local press report that you are to expand your UK operation in the coming year…'

When making a speculative approach to a company state your *generic* career goals. Write that you want to be considered for administration opportunities, for example, rather than, say, a job as a purchase ledger clerk. If too specific and there are no vacancies for the exact role, then your approach will be automatically rejected. On the other hand, don't ask to be considered for any kind of job within the company because nobody will know which manager should consider your letter.

Be assertive without being overbearingly pushy. State 'I look forward to meeting you soon', rather than 'I hope to hear from you in due course.' Ask for an interview or for a meeting.

Presentation

As with all job-getting documents, the presentation of your letter must be first-class. Nothing less is good enough for you. Always produce your letters on a word processor or typewriter unless an advertisement specifically asks for a *handwritten* response. A poorly handwritten letter on cheap paper can ruin your job application.

Paper

Always use one side only of one sheet of white or cream, good quality A4 paper.

Font

Your self-marketing approach will look more professional and effective if both the self-marketing letter and your CV use the same typeface.

Grammar and readability

Perfect grammar does not always equate to a readable document. Read your letter aloud to detect any mistakes or badly constructed sentences. If in doubt, ask someone to check it and accept constructive criticism.

Staples and paper clips

Remember that the recipient may need to photocopy your CV and send it to other managers. A wire staple makes this a chore and usually results in a ripped document. On the other hand, there is a risk of unattached documents being inadvertently left in the envelope or becoming separated and mislaid. It is therefore best to attach your CV and application form to the letter with a paper clip.

An example of a self-marketing letter is given in Figure 11.1.

SELF-MARKETING LETTER CHECKLIST

An effective self-marketing letter should:

- display your full address, postcode and telephone number(s);
- conform to a standard business letter style of presentation;
- be addressed to a named manager, quoting his or her preferred title and correct job title;
- not start with the word 'I';
- use bullet points to highlight your *Prime Selling Points*;
- convey enthusiasm and motivation;
- ask for a meeting or interview;
- be attached with a paper clip to your CV or application form;
- be sent unfolded, in an A4-sized envelope with a first-class postage stamp.

Make sure that a copy of each self-marketing letter is saved in your files along with a copy of the application form and/or CV that it accompanied.

Figure 11.1 Example of a self-marketing letter

12 Moor Lane
Honicknowle
Plymouth
PL5 2UU

Telephone: 01752 208048 (Home)
01752 778653 (Work)

2 August 200X

Ms Janet Potter
Admin/Personnel Manager
New World Professional Publishing
Moles Court
Berry Hill
Oxford
OX3 7EY

Dear Ms Potter

Ref. 100 – Regional Directors, Asia and Europe

Your advertisement in *The Times* (1 August) is of tremendous interest to me as the described role combines both my marketing and linguistic expertise. I can also offer proven ability in building and motivating successful sales teams, and feel that I can make a significant contribution on your behalf. A CV is enclosed in support of my application, and the following points seem especially relevant:

- Proven ability in successfully managing an international territory, directing a team of sales and marketing professionals within a world-wide blue-chip company.
- MBA qualified with successful experience in a very demanding commercial environment.
- Multilingual with proven ability in multicultural environments. Currently Marketing Manager for the Central European Region, involving extensive liaison with staff and customers at all corporate levels.
- Successful experience as a key member of a trans-European management team controlling and driving a brand-leading European product line.

I am particularly attracted by this opportunity to use my experience and skills in this field, and would certainly relish the new challenges offered by New World. I request a meeting to discuss the matter at the earliest opportunity, and I look forward to meeting you.

Yours sincerely

Helga Morgan
Enc.

Chapter 12

Using employment agencies

EMPLOYMENT AGENCIES ARE A SIGNIFICANT FACTOR IN THE JOB MARKET. THIS CHAPTER DISCUSSES THE ISSUES INVOLVED AND SHOWS HOW YOU CAN USE EMPLOYMENT AGENCIES TO GOOD EFFECT IN YOUR JOB SEARCH.

HE WHO PAYS THE PIPER CALLS THE TUNE?

An employment agency is a private company with the purpose of finding work for individuals. That is the definition adopted here, anyway. On the other hand, it may be argued that the purpose of an employment agency is to find suitable employees for their client companies. It is a question of emphasis. They themselves do not have any jobs to offer; they merely act as brokers between employers and job-seekers. Their agents constantly liaise with companies and organisations, asking to be allowed to submit candidates for their vacancies, and many major companies resort to their services. Employment agencies are a significant factor in the job market. No serious job-seeker can afford to ignore employment agencies and your job-search plan should include registration and regular contacts with carefully selected agencies. This chapter should be read in conjunction with Chapter 7 which dealt with online resources because virtually every employment agency uses the Internet as a major business tool.

HOW EMPLOYMENT AGENCIES OPERATE

Employment agencies operate in many different ways. For example, they might be paid by a company to advertise its job vacancies, screen applicants and provide a list of suitable candidates. Or a company might ask the agency to find a person to match a precise job specification, sometimes without publicising the search. Some agencies will deal with companies on an ongoing basis. Others might approach employers, touting a list of suitable people on their books.

The agency arranges the job interviews, perhaps coaches the candidate a little and liaises with the employer behind the scenes. In the case of permanent employment, the agency charges a fee to a company for introducing a person subsequently employed by the client. This commission rate varies, but 17–20 per cent of the employee's first year's salary is typical. The candidate, of course, has no dealings with or knowledge concerning business arrangements between the employer and the agency.

TEMPORARY EMPLOYMENT

There is a trend towards the use of subcontracted labour supplied and largely managed by employment agencies. For example, some very large-scale workplaces are staffed almost entirely by workers who are employed by an employment agency. In other instances, temporary workers are obtained through agencies to supplement the permanent workforce during peak periods or times of unexpected staff shortage. In virtually all of these cases, the agency will be responsible for all payroll matters concerning temporary workers, including PAYE tax and NI contributions; in turn, the agency submits an invoice to the employer, typically with a mark-up of 100 to 200 per cent. This mark-up may seem quite high, but it must be remembered that the agency has to cover overheads such as premises, marketing, advertising and recruitment consultants.

The world of work in the UK is changing. It must be accepted that temporary work is now an integral part of this world. This, of course, includes jobs at all levels, and interim management contracts are increasingly prevalent. Many employers firstly engage new staff on a temporary basis and then recruit proven people to their permanent staff (this is known as 'temp to perm' in the jargon of the recruitment industry). On this basis, they will often contract a local employment agency to handle fairly large and ongoing recruitment projects.

Other temporary jobs are short-term with little hope of ever being converted to permanent roles. However, it must be asked just what kind of job can be regarded as permanent in this changing world of work?

When considering temporary work:

▨ Check how you will be paid – weekly or monthly.

▨ Make sure you know the rate for the job.

▨ Check whether NI contributions will be paid for you.

▨ Ask regarding the arrangements for income tax.

▨ Find out how this might affect your Jobseekers Allowance and/or any other benefits.

When using an employment agency, remember the following important points:

■ The employing company pays the fee.

■ It is illegal in the UK for an employment agency to demand payment from a job-seeker.

Do not pay any money for enrolment, registration or anything else connected with an employment agency's activities in the job market on your behalf. If you encounter anything of this nature, you should report the agency to the Department of Trade and Industry.

Some agencies offer a CV-writing service, for which they can legitimately charge a fee. Do not be browbeaten into using such a service if you do not feel it necessary. They could be useful, however, if you have no word processor facilities. Agencies are not necessarily experts in CV preparation, and you are usually better to advised to rely on your own draft document.

DIFFERING QUALITY OF AGENCIES

Many agencies are excellent, some are adequate, some are mediocre and a few can be unscrupulous. Unfortunately, it is not easy to distinguish the good from the bad. A job-seeker who registers with an agency becomes part of that organisation's stock in hand. Some agencies have been known to advertise phantom vacancies ('jobs' which do not really exist) merely to attract a number of potentially valuable job-seekers onto its books. As agencies never reveal the name of their client companies, no individual is able to prove this abuse: the mystery job fades into the background in a cloud of excuses. However, the agency is left with a pile of marketable CVs.

EMPLOYMENT AGENCIES STANDARDS WATCHDOG

If you have any queries regarding an agency, or if you wish to make a complaint, you should contact the federal body of employment agencies:

Recruitment and Employment Confederation
36–38 Mortimer Street, London W1W 7RG
Tel: 020 7462 3260
Fax: 020 7255 2878
Website: http://www.rec.uk.com

The REC will provide advice and details regarding its members and their services. The body also has disciplinary powers over its members, up to and including expulsion.

Choosing your agencies

The quality of recruitment agencies varies tremendously. In the writer's experience this does not just apply from company to company, but also between different branches within the same company. While standardised procedures and policies will provide some consistency, so much depends upon the quality of individual branch managers and their staff. It is therefore necessary to be very selective when choosing your employment agencies. Do not necessarily confine yourself to agencies located in the immediate locality; many effective organisations have ongoing contacts with prospective employers (particularly large-scale national companies) covering a wide geographical area.

Make a list of potentially agencies by using the following sources:

- the Internet (see Chapter 7);

- Yellow Pages telephone book;

- your local library (ask for business and local authorities directories);

- the local and national newspapers (jobs sections);

- information from relatives and friends.

Make contact by telephone

Next, you should spend a morning contacting each agency by telephone. Initially, identify which agencies deal with the type of job that you are seeking. Many agencies specialise in specific areas (e.g. the engineering or science sectors) and there is little point in registering with an agency which has few if any dealings within your own field. If you have a computer, make up an agency database.

On the other hand, if the agency is situated a long way away, a purely exploratory trip will probably be out of the question. In these circumstances you will have to decide whether to send them your details through the mail or by Internet. If you do this, write a letter to accompany your skills list, making the ground rules clear: type of job sought, location, salary expectations, whether any application can be submitted without prior consultation with yourself. Note that the use of first names is the accepted practice in dealing with employment agencies (unlike when responding directly to employers).

DRAW UP A SHORTLIST

Eliminate the agencies which you deem to be unsuitable. Then look closely at your CV. Is it suitable for use by agencies? A lot will depend upon how widely you are casting your net in terms of sector, industry and kind of job. For employment agencies, a 'functional' CV format emphasising your range of key skills is more often effective than a CV which is structured around the jobs you have previously held. With agencies, as with employers, precisely target your CV at your goal. Look again at Chapters 9 and 10 before making up your mind.

MAKE UP A SKILLS LIST

Take a separate sheet of paper and draw up a brief marketing letter (see Figure 12.1). On a separate sheet list the skills you can offer to employers, together with a résumé of your employment history (see Figure 12.2). This is an initial discussion document to be used instead of your CV and does not provide vital information such as address, telephone number, etc. Produce a number of photocopies of this document.

PREPARE A LIST OF QUESTIONS

Decide the things that you need to know. Your questions might include:

- What types of vacancies/industries do they specialise in?
- How do they operate?
- Do they deal in permanent or temporary jobs, or both?
- If dealing in temporary jobs, do they pay holiday pay and/or sick pay?
- What possibilities are there for temporary jobs to become permanent after a certain time? And, in this event, what arrangements would apply between the agency and the employer?
- What types of jobs do they currently have on their books?
- What contact arrangements do they have with the people on their books?
- How do they feel about your CV?
- What suggestions do they have to include with your job-search plan?
- Will they contact you before submitting your details to a prospective employer?

Figure 12.1 A brief marketing letter

5 Arlsey Moor
Hillside
Morton Heysham
Devon
EX12 2DE

Tel 01724 345213

10 August 200X

Miss Mia Enderby
Search and Place Agency
High Street
Cookham
Buckinghamshire
SL7 6WQ

Dear Mia

Following our telephone conversation today, a short résumé of my skills and experience is enclosed for your information. I wish to relocate to the Maidenhead area, and would be available to commence my new position from 30 October onwards.

I am seeking an interesting and challenging post, either as a hands-on maintenance engineer or in a supervisory/managerial role. This would preferaby be within 30 minutes commuting distance of Maidenhead. My salary expectation would be in the range of £18,000–£22,000 p.a. (negotiable).

Please note that I do not wish my details to be forwarded to MacDuff Engineering, High Wycombe. However, I have no objections to you submitting my details to any other employers without prior discussion.

I can be contacted on the above telephone number, and look forward to hearing from you.

Yours sincerely

Richard Moss

Figure 12.2 Résumé of employment history

RICHARD MOSS   15 Hartley Gardens, Derby DE1 2TT   Tel. 01332 454407

ELECTRO-MECHANICAL MAINTENANCE FITTER with a wealth of varied experience achieved in different environments. Able to work across craft disciplines, using a flexible approach to resolve production problems as they arise at the workplace. Experience includes the **PLASTICS** industry, with knowledge of the maintenance and repair of **INJECTION MOULD** equipment. Very reliable and an exemplary time and attendance record.

SKILLS OFFERED

- Fault finding and rectification of a wide range of machines and equipment, including PLCs, CNCs, robotics, injection moulding machines, presses, lathes and ancillary equipment.

- Using a range of craft skills, including electrical, electronics, plumbing, pipe fitting, milling, turning, welding (CO^2 and ARC) and machine shop practices.

- Knowledge of pneumatics and hydraulics.

- Installing machinery and services, including three phase, air and water supplies.

- Small works repairs to the general fabric of the building, fixtures and fittings.

- Monitoring the water systems for purity and general health and safety.

- Complying with exacting ISO 9002 standards.

EMPLOYMENT HISTORY

1994 to date	Marapipe Ltd	ELECTRO-MECHANICAL MAINTENANCE FITTER
1992 to 1994	Permabright	MAINTENANCE FITTER
1985 to 1992	Self-employed	LIGHTING AND LASER TECHNICIAN
1981 to 1985	Permabright	APPRENTICE MAINTENANCE FITTER

LOCATION OF JOB SOUGHT

20 miles radius of Maidenhead, depending on salary.

VISIT THE AGENCIES

Make a personal visit to the agencies on your shortlist and judge the quality of their service for yourself. While this is not a real employment interview, you should take the trouble to be appropriately turned out. It may not be an occasion for 'best bib and tucker', but first impressions are still important. Recruitment consultants have to maintain their own reputations with client companies and they will try to submit a certain standard of candidate. If you turn up in your gardening clothes, it may colour the consultant's opinion against you.

THE INITIAL INTERVIEW

Ensure that the interview is private. Present the consultant with a copy of your skills list as a basis for discussion and ask if he or she is familiar with your type of work. Do not supply your address or telephone number at this stage. If asked, smile nicely and say that you are not yet certain whether you want to register with the agency but, if you finally decide to do so, then you will be obviously happy to provide the information. Do not be embarrassed at being forthright. Neither should you be deflected in your purpose.

Remember that this is a two-way transaction: you need to be sure that you are comfortable doing business with the agency. You should interview the recruitment consultant using your list of questions. Of course, the consultant will also want to interview you to see if you are a candidate they can usefully work with. Only when satisfied with the answers to your questions should you proceed to the next stage and hand over your CV.

FILLING IN AGENCY REGISTRATION FORMS

Many employment agencies will have their own document procedures and you may be required to fill in one of their forms. Usually, the terms and conditions are on the reverse of this form. It is a good idea to ask if you can fill it in it home and return it later. This gives you the time to consider any dubious questions and also to study the terms. If there is anything that you are unsure about then you should ask for clarification before registering.

COMPUTERISED RECORDS

In most cases nowadays, your details will be placed on a computerised database. Any organisation which maintains computerised records on individuals is subject to the Data Protection Act. You are entitled to see what information is being held about you. Should you have any suspicions, you can demand your right to inspect any computerised file which refers to you.

EMPLOYMENT AGENCY PROCEDURES

Make sure that you are clear about the methods of each employment agency you use. How will they deal with suitable vacancies when they arise?

Often, recruitment consultants prefer to use the telephone rather written correspondence. In either event, they should provide the fullest details possible. Use the checklist in Figure 12.3.

MAINTAINING CONTACT

Make sure that you maintain regular contact with each agency, either by personal visits or telephone calls. Do not expect the agency to frequently contact you with progress reports; if they do, then you can be pleasantly surprised. An example of a contact log is given in Figure 12.4.

Figure 12.3 Recruitment consultants checklist

- Name of the employer (It is common practice for the name of the company to be withheld in the early stages. The following information should be given, however.)
- Interview details:
  - panel or one to one
  - personnel manager/line manager
  - any tests (psychometric, ability, aptitude, etc.)
- Location and relevant details
- Information about the employer – nature of business:
  - size
  - turnover
  - no. of employees
- Job specification (Do not be fobbed off regarding a job description – the agency will invariably have one, or they could not have accepted the contract.)
- Main terms and conditions
- Salary range
- Other benefits (company car, health scheme, etc.)

Figure 12.4 Employment agency contact log

Agency ....   Date regististered ....

Address ....

....

Telephone no. ....   Fax no. ....

E-mail ....   Website URL ....

Consultants: ....

....

Date	Consultant	Notes	Follow-up date

SUMMARY OF ADVICE FOR USING AGENCIES

- Agencies may not know of every vacancy that exists in your target job-search sector, but they will certainly know of many more than you do. They frequently know of the best manager in a company to receive your CV and, more importantly, know how to get it to that person. So register with at least one carefully selected agency. Choose agencies by reputation and recommendation – talk to other people to get the facts.

- Decide how many agencies you want to use. This depends on your skills set and aspirations: often one agency is sufficient in a clearly defined and relatively narrow job market. On the other hand, if you are looking for a more general role with a wide range of possibilities, you would be better registering with a small number of agencies. Don't let the agencies know that you have registered with more than one because they are likely to be less inclined to spend time on your behalf. Do remember, too, that agencies tend to be competing in the same markets and an employer could well receive your CV from more than one source.

- Much of this book has been about job-search strategy. Discuss your strategy with your agent and get a view on whether he or she considers it realistic. If they think it unviable, you should not necessarily accept their verdict. Consider the view objectively and reject it if you still feel that you are on the right track (remember the different agendas attached to the three viewpoints). If you cannot agree on the strategy, you obviously need to go to another agency.

- When your strategy is communicated and agreed make sure that the agent follows it. Make it clear that you do not want your CV to be sent out just anywhere, and that you want to know where it has been sent. You can still allow the agency to use its expertise and specialist knowledge in selecting companies, but make sure that it is clear that you expect them to update you regularly with a record of where it has been sent.

- In any event, keep in regular contact with the agency. Experience shows that most agents respond to clients who are proactive and demanding. Be persistent, and if your agent can't take your call immediately, make sure that he or she rings you back.

- If the agent does not ring you back as a matter of practice, or if there are other areas for concern, then formally remove yourself from their books. Do not accept poor service or unprofessional behaviour. If necessary, report malpractice to the REC using the contact details provided earlier in this chapter.

Chapter 13 ▉
Job-searching

JOB SEARCH INVOLVES EFFECTIVE ADMINISTRATION AND ORGANISATION IN METHODI-
CALLY RESEARCHING YOUR CHOSEN JOB MARKETS. THIS CHAPTER PROVIDES THE
NECESSARY INFORMATION AND TOOLS.

A fundamental distinction is drawn here between job-searching and job-getting. The
former refers to locating available jobs, while the latter concerns the steps taken to
actually win job offers. They are two sides of the same coin. Both are equally important because the quality of either side will greatly affect the other.

Job-search involves effective administration and organisation in methodically
researching your chosen job markets:

- identifying sources of appropriate job vacancy advertisements;

- obtaining job bulletins from organisations;

- identifying potential employers in your selected job markets;

- finding relevant company names and addresses and building your database;

- starting to network – methodically listing your personal contacts and mobilising
  them.

Having already defined your target markets, it is now necessary to identify potential
employers and employment opportunities within those markets. This next stage of
our marketing process is divided into three separate operations:

- locating relevant job vacancy advertisements;

- building a list of relevant employers' names and addresses for direct speculative
  approaches;

- personal networking.

USE AND EFFECTIVENESS OF JOB SEARCH METHODS

A survey of a random sample of almost 75,000 jobseekers produced the results given
in Table 13.1.

Table 13.1 Effectivenss of job search methods

Method	Usage* %	Effectiveness Rate** %
Applied directly to employer	66.0	47.7
Asked friends about jobs where they work	50.8	22.1
Asked friends about jobs elsewhere	41.8	11.9
Asked relatives about jobs where they worked	28.4	19.3
Asked relatives about jobs elsewhere	27.3	7.4
Answered local newspaper advertisements	11.7	10.0
Private employment agency	21.0	24.2
State employment service	33.5	13.7
School placement officer	12.5	21.4
Civil Service test	15.3	12.5
Asked school/college/university tutor	10.4	12.1
Went to place where employers come to pick up staff	1.4	8.2
Placed advertisement in local paper	1.6	12.9
Placed advertisement in non-local paper	0.5	–
Answered advertisements in professional/trade journals	4.9	7.3
Contacted local organisation	5.6	12.7
Placed advertisements in professional/trade journals	0.6	–
Other	11.8	39.7

* Percentage of total jobseekers using this method.
** A percentage obtained by dividing the number of job-seekers who found work in this way by the total number who used the method.

SCANNING THE 'SITUATIONS VACANT' COLUMNS

It is important to make sure that you trawl through every relevant newspaper and magazine to unearth advertisements for suitable job vacancies. Cast your net widely, incorporating both local and national publications. Do not neglect the local and national specialist publications which are solely devoted to recruitment, available from most newsagents. You should also make a point of searching out trade journals and publications from professional bodies in your chosen target job markets.

Your town library will have copies of most newspapers and magazines if you decide not to buy them. If you do choose to use library resources, use your job schedule to make a list of the issues you need to study, and be prepared to photocopy any relevant advertisements.

Remember to include free newspapers and local magazines which are delivered to all homes in most areas. This is an economical and effective advertising medium for recruiters, and therefore a rich vein of job vacancies.

Using the chart provided in Figure 13.1, make a comprehensive list of the newspapers and publications you intend to monitor. This chart already shows various relevant publications and the days they are issued. Delete and amend as necessary, according to your personal needs, and add local publications to produce your own

Figure 13.1 Job advertising reading list

Monday	Tuesday	Wednesday	Thursday	Friday	Weekly	Monthly
Guardian Creative Media Marketing	*Independent* Accountancy City Appointments General	*Daily Telegraph* Sales Media Marketing	*Daily Telegraph* Appointments Supplement (Executive)	*Guardian* Computing Science & Technology General	*Job Search* Many IT jobs, but also engineering and general	
Independent Computing	*The Times* Health Care Legal Public Sector	*Financial Times* Banking, Finance General Management	*Financial Times* Accountancy	*Independent* Legal	*Jobs South East*	
The Times Education Supplement Secretarial		*Guardian* Education	*Guardian* Social Services Finance Personnel		*The Grocer Magazine* Jobs in Sales, Marketing and Retail (not always confined to Grocery trade)	
		Independent Creative Marketing Media Sales	*Independent* Education Public Sector General Graduate Opportunities			
		The Times Creative, Marketing Media 'Crème de la Crème' Secretarial & Office Appointments	*The Times* General Management Appointments Supplement			

weekly job advertisement reading list. Then take immediate steps to make sure that you see the latest on a *regular* basis.

Photocopy or cut out any advertisements that attract your attention. Paste these onto A4 sheets and keep them in a plastic wallet making sure that you also note the name and date of the publication. Cross reference your file with an entry in your job-search log for each vacancy.

BUILDING YOUR EMPLOYER DATABASE

The next step is to search out the names and addresses of employers in each of the job markets you are targeting. Build a personal database of company addresses, including those gleaned from the Internet and directories, and also those obtained from the 'Situations Vacant' columns of newspapers and adverts which do *not* refer to your kind of job.

When a company is recruiting it is a reasonable indicator that the business is doing well. It is also likely that they may need other kinds of staff in the near future. Newspaper advertisements usually include the name of an appropriate personnel, human resources or line manager, the full postal address and postcode. Address your own enquiry to the named manager, without mentioning the original advertisement. Delay your approach for a couple of weeks – the manager is not then immediately aware how you found his or her name and can be intrigued enough to see you.

The aim is to list all companies and organisations with which you would like to find a job. This is hard work but it is an ongoing task and can largely be done in manageable stages when you have time to spare. There are a number of places to find these addresses.

Trade directories

There is a wide range of commercial and trade directories, most of which are stocked in most town libraries. Not only do they provide addresses of potential employers in particular locations and trade sectors, they also offer a wealth of other information, such as the names of directors and senior managers, the number of people employed, other offices and so on.

The following publications can be used:

- *Key British Enterprises*
- *Kompass* – UK and Ireland
- *Kelly's Business Directory*

- *Personnel Managers Year Book*

- *The Stock Exchange Official Year Book*

- *The Financial Times Top 1000*

- *Who Owns Whom*

- *Directory of Directors*.

Yellow Pages, Thompsons and local directories

Telephone and local directories should not be ignored. They conveniently arrange lists of companies according to trade and industry, although they do not provide managers' names and the postcode is usually omitted. You can always telephone and ask for this information.

Local authority and chamber of commerce directories

Many local authorities produce directories that list business concerns in their area. Usually, these lists are free of charge, although there does seem to be a trend for more and more councils to charge for them or subcontract the work to a private company. The presentation and content of local authority directories differs widely, but they often include useful details such as number employed, trade sector and sometimes managers' names. It is always worth making telephone calls to councils in areas where you are interested in working – ask for the council's Economic Development Department as a starting point.

Virtually every Chamber of Commerce produces a comprehensive directory of its member companies. These usually provide excellent information, but they are expensive to buy. However, these organisations are often very helpful and sympathetic towards pro-active job searchers, and it is sometimes possible to get a free copy of the previous year's directory. Alternatively, the local library may keep a copy.

Newspapers and magazines

The news media provides an excellent source of company addresses. Every job advertisement indicates some movement within an organisation, whether or not it refers to your own particular field. The very fact that a company is recruiting is often a sign that it is doing well, and there is a possibility of other job opportunities there.

Also, of course, job advertisements provide the full name, address and telephone number of the company. Furthermore, many also give the name of an appropriate personnel, HR or line manager. It is a good idea to save old newspapers and magazines just for this purpose; whenever you have some spare time, go through them and collect the information for your database.

Editorial pieces and business sections can give you some ideas for potential openings in companies. Scan the pages for news of expansions, relocations, new branches and so on. Then find the address of the company or organisation by consulting trade directories or telephoning the head office. Add these addresses to your database too, with a note of the activity that first attracted your attention (for later use in the speculative approach letter).

COMPILING YOUR EMPLOYER DATABASE

Draw up and photocopy a blank database sheet. This also provides a template for the fields of a computerised database if you are using one. Note that the page also provides a reference sheet to log your activities and enable you to keep track of your job-search activities.

If you have the facilities, it is strongly recommended that you compile a computerised database. This is a great boon when you start sending speculative letters to each of the employers on your target list. However, it is also advisable to keep paper records as shown in Figure 13.2 – they are more portable and readily accessible. Besides which, the database sheets have more than one purpose, and will be invaluable when you are preparing for an interview following a successful contact.

SUMMARY OF STEPS TO MAKE YOUR DATABASE

1. Go to the library and ask for the relevant directories for your target job markets. Look at both the trade sector and geographical area listings. It is recommended that you start with *Kompass* and *Key British Enterprises*. Also look in the directories issued by local authorities and chambers of commerce. Also look in *Yellow Pages* and *Thompson's* local directories

2. Transcribe or photocopy the selected names and addresses, using the record sheet as a template for information. Note down any potentially useful information such as products, other branches, etc.

3. Obtain both current and past editions of newspapers and magazines. Cull the names and addresses of companies and organisations advertising in the jobs columns.

4. Note the names of companies mentioned in editorials and business sections. Locate the addresses and details, and add them to your database.

5. If appropriate to your job markets, drive, cycle or walk around industrial and trading estates, noting suitable names and addresses.

Figure 13.2 Employer database

Target job market	
Company/ organisation name	
Address 1	
Address 2	
District	
Town/city	

County		Postcode	
Telephone no.		Fax no.	
Manager's first name		Manager's second name	
Job title		E-mail address	
Source of information		No. of employees	Date of source

Notes

Date of approach	Date of 1st follow-up	Date of 2nd follow-up
Response	Response	Response

6. Write to trade associations and institutes and ask for details of suitable companies. Transcribe the information to your database.

7. File your database sheets in alphabetical order divided into Target Job Markets.

8. If you are using a computerised database, input the information for each company.

Get as many addresses as you can. Do not limit your search for potential employers. You may feel that it is better to concentrate on larger companies as there is a better chance that vacancies exist when you approach them. On the other hand, changes in the world of work have meant a decline in the number of large-scale workplaces. Ninety-five per cent of the UK workforce is now employed by companies of less than 100 employees, and the largest growth is in companies of less than 20 employees. Smaller companies are often more likely to respond to direct approaches as their recruitment practices are usually more flexible than large organisations with established procedures. Besides, you may be able to get in 'at the ground floor' and grow with the company. So you should not ignore the small businesses.

PERSONAL NETWORKING

Networking is a term that is commonly used but not always understood. It refers to mobilising your own personal contacts, both to gain personal referrals to employers and to obtain valuable information, e.g. details of possible job opportunities, managers' names, etc.

Everyone uses a personal referral system for all manner of things in their daily lives. If you need a builder, for example, do you look in the local newspaper for an advert or do you ask friends if they can recommend someone? A reliable plumber, sympathetic doctors, a suitable cattery, helpful accountant …. You can easily find a list of advertised services, but you can only get some idea of their quality by talking to other experienced users. In ordinary life, we take such networking for granted. In fact, in every aspect of our life, we all rely upon personal recommendations from people whom we feel can be trusted. That is networking. It is a fashionable word for something that we all do as a matter of course.

The same approach is invaluable in your job-search system. So try to establish a network of people who know your worth and who have good contacts. If you haven't already done so, you should begin and maintain a networking record which lists the following contacts:

- colleagues who now work for other employers;

- associates working with suppliers you have dealt with;

- representatives of customers and clients who know your work;

- trainers and tutors;

- professional bodies, institutes and trade unions;

- friends and 'friends of friends';

- relatives.

NETWORKING CHECKLIST

Everybody uses networking in their day-to-day relationships, and yet many people have difficulty in deliberately using it in their job-search. People like to help. You are genuinely complimenting friends by asking for their assistance. Networking is not an abuse of friendship if exercised with courtesy, dignity and respect. The following guidelines should be useful:

- Make a list of friends and acquaintances who might be able to help you by giving information about vacancies. You are not asking them to get you a job; if they offer a direct referral, that is a bonus. Use every contact that you can think of.

- Systematically get in touch with the people on your list, either by meeting them, telephoning or writing. Tick your list as you make each contact.

- Make it clear that your approach is part of a methodical job-search programme, demonstrating that you are taking responsibility for your own destiny.

- Tell each person about the sorts of job you that are looking for, and ask him or her to be on the lookout for any similar opportunities.

- Only use flattery if you genuinely mean it: 'You have a lot of good contacts…' or 'You meet a lot of people from different companies…'

- Respect the confidentiality of your contacts when following up their leads.

- When speaking to your contacts, ask about their own situation, encourage them to look at the job markets and offer to pass any suitable leads to them. More to the point, *do it* – networking is about giving as well as receiving.

Some don'ts

- Don't be too proud to use methodical networking techniques.

- Don't ask the impossible and make people feel useless.

- Don't ask people to do things that might embarrass them.

- Don't embarrass people by asking them directly to give you a job.

- Don't ask anyone to get a job for you.

- Don't get too absorbed in your own world – remember to ask about the welfare of your friends.

SUMMARY

This chapter has covered a wide range of important research and self-marketing activities. These are separate activities that must be ongoing, and conscientiously undertaken *simultaneously* throughout your job-getting campaign. It requires dedication, self-discipline and hard work, but the quality of this groundwork greatly affects the success of your effort.

Chapter 14

Getting into the marketplace

THE PREVIOUS CHAPTER EXPLAINED HOW TO LOCATE AND COLLECT RELEVANT ADVER-TISEMENTS AND JOB VACANCY DETAILS. WE NEXT CONCENTRATE ON PREPARING AN EFFECTIVE AND WINNING RESPONSE.

It is time for action at the cutting edge of your job-getting campaign: placing relevant applications into viable and appropriate job markets. This means as many quality applications as possible! There is a law of averages, and it applies to job-getting as much as to anything else: the more applications that you have in play at any one time, the more chances of success you will have. Also, effort generates its own energy, and it multiplies at an exponential rate. Any job-searcher is more stimulated by ongoing activities, by letters dropping onto the doormat, by preparation for interviews, telephoning and talking to prospective employers, talking to employment agencies...

A word of warning may be timely here: do not invest all of your hopes and expectations in any one job vacancy. A particular job can appear to be exciting and enticing, seeming to offer everything that you are seeking. It may seem to 'have your name written on it'. The temptation is to apply for this job and then to suspend any other job-getting activity. This can obviously cause other valuable opportunities to be neglected. Also, if the application is ultimately unsuccessful, it can deal a great blow to your self-confidence and self-esteem. It is so much better to have plenty of other job applications in the selection process at the same time, giving every cause for optimism even if one of them fails.

In the process of getting into the job marketplaces, we begin with job vacancy advertisements. The previous chapter explained how to locate and collect relevant advertisements. We next concentrate on analysing the advertisement and preparing an effective and winning response.

Figure 14.1 Job vacancy information sheet

Company	Name of manager
Address	Telephone
	Fax
	E-mail
Job title	Salary
Advertisement source	Date of advertisement
	Date of application
EMPLOYERS' REQUIREMENTS	**PERSONAL SKILLS & EXPERIENCE**
KEY COMPETENCIES REQUIRED	**PRIME SELLING POINTS**
Notes	
Date of Employer's Response	Result

ANALYSING ADVERTISEMENTS

An essential skill in using the Globeskills PSP job-getting system is the ability to analyse advertisements to identify *Key Competencies Required* for each job, enabling you then to choose your *Prime Selling Points* for this application.

The previous chapter recommended that all selected advertisements are clipped or photocopied, pasted to A4 paper and filed in plastic wallets in your job-getting folder. Always make a note of the name and date of the publication.

Job vacancy advertisements usually have up to six elements:

- company information (the blurb);
- job information;
- details of terms and conditions (salary etc.);
- essential requirements;
- desirable requirements;
- method of application.

A well-written advertisement will be a concise and easily read 'shopping list' of the employer's requirements, but others need the perception of a clairvoyant to identify the needs of the job (the *Key Competencies Required*, in PSP terms).

When analysing an advertisement, read it carefully a couple of times first. You may even find conflicting messages in the advertisement. Do not let this put you off, but note your observation: it may indicate that the specification is the work of more than one person, each of whom has slightly different views on the nature of the job.

This section uses the example of an actual job vacancy (see Figure 14.2). The fictitious character 'John Collins', created to illustrate CV production in a previous chapter, will again be used to demonstrate the *Prime Selling Points* system.

The following step-by-step approach will pay dividends:

1. Treat each selected advertisement as a separate project. Read it carefully to make sure that it fits into your job-search plans. Is it within one of your target job markets? If not and the job still appeals to you, it is probable that the job market should be added to your target list.

2. Use a highlighter pen to emphasise the employer's requirements.

3. Assess which requirements are *essential* and which are *desirable*. Also, make a note of any important competencies for job that are not included but which you think may be needed. (It is often necessary to 'second-guess' when considering poorly worded adverts.)

Figure 14.2 Example of a job vacancy

national aids trust
leading partnerships to fight HIV

NAT is an independent charity established in 1987 in support of the responses to HIV & AIDS. We aim to initiate, develop and support efforts to prevent the spread of HIV and to improve the quality of life for people with HIV and AIDS throughout the UK.

IT OFFICER
(part time – 21 hours per week)
Salary: £10k – £14k (incl. London Weighting) depending upon experience and qualifications; Initial 1-year contract

NAT requires someone to be responsible for the general running and development of its computer system. NAT has on average 15 staff, most full-time, some part-timers and others operating from home.

You will look after the Ethernet networked PC system (Macs), assist with the development of databases (FileMaker Pro), liaise with software consultants, assist with the development of the NAT website, and have a 'hands-on' role in supporting staff to operate to maximum efficiency including some training.

You will be experienced in supporting and managing a network, web-site maintenance and Microsoft Office 98 Applications.

You will have the ability to advise on improvements to current IT practices within the organisation.

For full details of the post, please send a post card quoting the job title, together with you name and address to:

National AIDS Trust, New City Cloisters, 188/196 Old Street, London EC1V 9FR

Closing date for applications: Thursday, 21 January 1999

Interviews: Friday 29 January 1999.

NAT is striving towards equal opportunities and particularly encourages applications from women and black and minority ethnic communities. We also particularly welcome applications for people living with HIV.

NATIONAL
LOTTERY
CHARITIES
BOARD

The National AIDS Trust is a Registered Charity No: 297977

---

4. List all of the requirements in one column of your job vacancy information sheet. Include all of the identified points, even if you do not possess a particular attribute; this helps when considering ways of tackling any deficiencies in the job application.

In the example of the IT job shown in Figure 14.2 a long list emerges. Some of these are more important than others, of course, and by no means all of them can be classed as *Key Competencies Required*. However, even the less important points will play a supporting role in the application:

■ General running and development of computer system

■ Full- and part-time staff – some working at home

■ Ethernet networked Mac computers

- Filemaker Pro databases

- Liaising with software consultants

- Knowledge of website development and maintenance

- IT support experience in a large organisation

- Knowledge in training other staff

- Experience in managing a network

- Knowledge of Microsoft Office applications

- Able to advise on IT systems.

Let us suppose that John Collins does not have experience either in Filemaker Pro databases or in Mac computers. He is, however, well versed in other database systems, and has a good knowledge of novel local area networks.

5. Making an informed judgement, select the four or five *Key Competencies Required* at the core of the job. Mark your job vacancy information sheet (Figure 14.1) accordingly.

In our National Aids Trust example, the following *Key Competencies Required* have been identified:

- Good IT knowledge

- Knowledge of Microsoft Office applications

- Experience in supporting and managing a network

- Able to undertake website maintenance

- Ability to provide IT support to staff (possibly non-computer-literate).

Additionally, the following desirable requirements are noted. They are not absolutely essential, but possessing these attributes in addition to the main needs of the job could tip the balance in a candidate's favour:

- Knowledge of Ethernet networked PC systems – Macs

- Experienced in liaising with software consultants

- Experience in using FileMaker Pro databases.

6. Consider any of the *Key Competencies Required* which you do *not* possess, e.g. qualifications, language ability, physical attributes and so on. Ask yourself if this really disqualifies you from applying. As a general rule, if you can satisfy more than half of the requirements and there is no obvious debarring factor, then apply anyway.

Clearly, there are some drawbacks in John Collins' application. He has no experience in Filemaker Pro databases, for example, although he does know about other databases. (However, most serious candidates for a job such as this will probably be experienced in using a comparable database system.) Equally, using IBM-compatible PCs rather than Macs may be a drawback, but it does not disqualify skills in the networking of PCs. It will be necessary to mitigate these potential negatives and also to make the most of positive points to outweigh them.

7. Select your four or five *Prime Selling Points*, as far as possible mirroring the *Key Competencies Required*. Choose a snappy form of words to encapsulate these PSPs (combining two *Key Competencies Required* in one bulleted *Prime Selling Point* is good practice). Note these on your job vacancy information sheet. Take particular care at this stage because the selected PSPs will form the whole basis for your job getting tactics, including setting the agenda for the subsequent interview.

Returning the our National Aids Trust example, the following *Prime Selling Points* have been chosen:

- Extensive experience in the IT industry, with a strong background in providing effective IT support to large organisations.

- Proven ability in the development and management of local area networked PC systems.

- Wide knowledge and expertise in using Microsoft Office applications, including the development of interactive, multi-relational databases.

- Innovative approach to providing web services – designed, evaluated and maintained an award-winning road safety site on behalf of a UK police authority.

Note that no mention is made of the applicant's lack of experience in using Mac computers, although great emphasis is placed upon the experience in networked PCs. Similarly, the Filemaker Pro weakness is mitigated with a strong reference to databases which suggests a good knowledge of the subject. Note also how the *Prime Selling Point* concerning website skills is illustrated with a powerful example.

There are some other, minor attributes possessed by our fictitious candidate that are not strong enough for a PSP but which could usefully be included in the CV: liaising with contractors and training non-computer-literate staff, for example.

Steps 5 and 7 are emphasised because these are the key elements in the whole PSP system. The very essence of any successful job-getting method is matching the employer's needs with the things that you can personally offer, and then successfully presenting and selling those valued attributes.

The next step, therefore, is to customise your job-getting documents to highlight and emphasise the fact that you have got the key skills and qualities that the employer is seeking with the advertisement.

TAILORING YOUR CV

Having decided what your *Prime Selling Points* are going to be for any given vacancy, you should now look closely at your CV to make sure that they are prominently displayed and demonstrated.

Construct a new profile which incorporates each of the *Prime Selling Points*. This is your banner headline – a short and effective 'commercial advertisement' which proclaims how well you meet the main needs of this particular job. One paragraph will be enough, and certainly no more than two. It is permissible to use bold type to highlight each separate point in the short narrative.

Having made the claim in the profile, you must ensure that it is supported by emphasising each of your *Prime Selling Points* in the bulleted statements on the first page of your CV. They should be prominent in the first 6 to 8 inches of the page.

If you lack any particular *Key Competency Required*, try to mitigate the omission with a supporting bullet point that indicates some ability in that direction, and also by giving extra weight to one of the other *Prime Selling Points* where you excel.

Finally, go through the job vacancy information sheet and try to include statements which demonstrate that you can meet each of the subsidiary requirements. Include those points which have not been mentioned in the advertisement but which you judge to be important.

This may seem like an extensive rewriting of your CV but, in practice, if it is originally targeted to the specific job market, you will find that relatively minor changes are required. In fact, your CV will gradually evolve and become more sharply honed as you incorporate and emphasise skills that are highly sought after.

IMPLANTING *PRIME SELLING POINTS*

INTO YOUR CAREER HISTORY

First of all, review your library resource CV. Print the rambling document in its entirety, *and be prepared to edit it ruthlessly*. Remember that the bulk of your material should be recent rather than wasting space on experience gained 20 years ago.

1. Start in the body of the CV with the bulleted points that describe your experience and skills as demonstrated in your last/most recent job. Are there any that can be amended to describe one of the selected *Prime Selling Points* for the job you are targeting? Some may match almost exactly, of course. Tick those points that are likely to be used.

2. Eliminate any points that are irrelevant for this job, no matter how fond you are of them and despite the fact they will probably be useful for other job applications. The aim of the PSP system is to focus tightly on the recruiter's requirements for this job – anything else is merely wasting valuable space

3. Carefully amend the selected statements to give positive and upbeat examples that really strongly press the claims of each of your *Prime Selling Points*.

4. If necessary, write new bulleted statements to demonstrate any of your *Prime Selling Points* that remain to be covered.

5. When this has been done, rearrange the order of the bulleted statements to ensure that the *Prime Selling Points* are at the top of the list.

6. Go through the remaining points to see which of them can be eliminated in order to make the presentation fit nicely onto the front page. Only widen page margins or reduce print size as an absolute last resort.

Customising your personal profile

The profile is particularly useful for strongly highlighting your strengths for *this* job. Furthermore, it is the banner headline and introduction, and sets the tone for the reader from the outset. With a little practice, it is relatively easy to virtually rewrite the advertisement, making the same points but using different words, thus ensuring that you satisfy the employer's 'shopping list'.

This calculated exercise in 'mirroring' the employer is not dishonest. You are not fabricating falsehoods, but merely promoting those of your attributes that especially match the needs of the job. Quite obviously, this is bound to be more effective than a general CV that is used for every kind of job application.

Other factors

Look at the job titles that you have used for previous jobs. Do they adequately reflect the nature of the position that you are now seeking? If not, then it is permissible to change them within reason. This is often necessary anyway, because many formal job titles do not begin to describe the nature of the work to a third party. There is no reason why you must use a title that was, after all, someone else's invention: you are concerned with impressing a recruiter, not an ex-employer. It is important to ensure that the title you choose reflects the work that you did, however.

It is sometimes a good idea to promote your major qualification to your front page if it is especially needed for the job. Alternatively, you can allude to it in the profile: 'Graduate IT specialist...'

Finally, make sure that everything fits onto two pages, and print off the result on your best quality paper. Which of the bulleted selling points have the potential to become *Prime Selling Points* for this job? Make sure that you save the specially tailored CV with the copy of your marketing letter. This will form a vital part of your interview preparation. Also note your application in your job-getting log.

WRITING YOUR TARGETED SELF-MARKETING LETTER

This is a surprisingly easy task. The main part of your letter, comprising the bulleted *Prime Selling Points*, has already been written. Using the technique described in Chapter 11, it is now only necessary to write the opening 'Tempter' and concluding 'Action' paragraphs.

The following would be a suitable 'Tempter' paragraph for the example job application by John Collins:

> *My skills and experience closely match the requirements described by your advertisement in The Guardian (2 January), and I believe that I can make a significant contribution on your behalf. My CV is enclosed, and the following strengths are emphasised in support of my application: ...*

That is all that is needed for the opening paragraph! In fact any more detail can be self-defeating. This minimalist style serves its purpose in intriguing the reader and inviting him or her to read on.

Your bulleted *Prime Selling Points* can now be added without alteration. These are the things that the letter is really about: the rest is gift-wrapping.

The Action paragraph can be brief too:

> *These qualities would, I feel, be of value in this role, and I am particularly attracted by the chance to develop IT practices and train others to the benefit of the Trust. My experience in liaising with software consultants and in developing effective websites would, I feel, be valuable in this respect. I would welcome the opportunity of an interview and look forward to meeting you.*

Note the inclusion of supporting selling points in the final paragraph. Sign off with 'Yours sincerely'.

All that is now required is to add the name and address of the candidate and the recipient in the prescribed manner. Note that the example advertisement does not supply either the appropriate manager's name or job title; it is necessary to telephone for these details and add them to the letter as shown in Figure 14.3.

Figure 14.3 Self-marketing letter

33 Newfoundland Way
Berkhamsted
Hertfordshire
HP4 7LZ

Tel: 01422 556789
E-mail: jcollins@patrol.i-way.co.uk

3 January 200X

Mr Gordon Hollingsworth
National Organiser
National Aids Trust
New City Cloisters
188/196 Old Street
London EC1V 9FR

Dear Mr Hollingsworth

IT Officer

My skills and experience closely match the requirements described by your advertisement in *The Guardian* (2 January), and I believe that I can make a significant contribution on your behalf. My CV is enclosed, and the following strengths are emphasised in support of my application:

- Extensive experience in the IT industry, with a strong background in providing effective IT support to large organisations.

- Proven ability in the development and management of local area networked PC systems.

- Wide knowledge and expertise in using Microsoft Office applications, including the development of interactive, multi-relational databases.

- Innovative approach to providing web services – designed, evaluated and maintained an award-winning road safety site on behalf of a UK police authority.

These qualities would, I feel, be of value in this role, and I am particularly attracted by the chance to develop IT practices and train others to the benefit of the Trust. My experience in liaising with software consultants and in developing effective websites would, I feel, be valuable in this respect. I would welcome the opportunity of an interview and look forward to meeting you.

Yours sincerely

John Collins

Print off your *targeted* self-marketing letter and attach it to the tailored CV, slip it inside a large A4 envelope and add a first-class stamp. Finally, mark the envelope 'Private and Confidential'. The task is completed, and a *targeted* job application is on its way with a real chance of winning an interview. (The repeated emphasis is intended to drive home the need to customise your documentation to each specific job, and thereby greatly improve your prospects of success.)

This process can be applied to any advertised job vacancy. To summarise, the essential steps are:

1. Analyse the advertisement.

2. Identify the requirements of the job.

3. Select the main *Key Competencies Required* from the list.

4. Select your *Prime Selling Points* to match the *Key Competencies Required*.

5. Write sharp bulleted statements marketing each of your *Prime Selling Points*.

6. Customise your CV to included the *Prime Selling Points*.

7. Write your self-marketing letter, with the body comprised of the bulleted statements which market your *Prime Selling Points*.

8. Save both a hard copy and, where appropriate, a computer file of both the targeted CV and self-marketing letter. (It is important to know exactly what you have said when using this method!)

9. Note the details of the application in your job-getting log.

Chapter 15

Filling in application forms

YOU WILL ALWAYS PRODUCE AN EFFECTIVE AND POSITIVE APPLICATION FORM BY TAKING THE STEPS OUTLINED IN THIS CHAPTER.

In the Globeskills method, the application form is viewed as an opportunity rather than an irksome task. It will be apparent that this involves using a targeted approach to filling in application forms. It centres upon marketing your *Prime Selling Points* and tries to leave nothing to chance. You will always produce an effective and positive application by taking the steps outlined in this chapter.

Few people like filling in application forms. Some forms are small booklets and answering the questions can often occupy a whole evening and beyond. Nevertheless, application forms are here to stay. If you want to work for some companies, they are unavoidable. More and more companies use application forms nowadays. There are many reasons for this, most of them concerning a need for standardisation. Most companies use computerised records and this requires data in a set format. Some organisations use computer scanners to electronically store information, and this requires standard forms. Enlightened recruitment policies require that candidates are given equal opportunities, and a consistency in methods of application fall within that. The drive towards consistent and controlled procedures has produced a need for information to be collated in a structured format.

So there are good reasons why employers use an application form, although this does not explain why one is obliged to cram in a lengthy training record, for example, into a very small box. Or why a whole page is devoted to your health record and comprises a 'Yes or No' checklist of chronic and often rare illnesses. This, however, may give some indication of the culture and priorities of the organisation.

The onus is upon you to present the best case in highlighting your best selling points. You should view an application form as a means of impressing recruiters and persuading them that you must be given an interview. More than that, it is an opportunity to promote your *Prime Selling Points*.

All forms demand a great deal of thought. Make sure that you have the job vacancy advertisement and, if applicable, the job specification to hand before you start because these are virtually shopping lists of the employer's needs. Analyse the job and decide your *Prime Selling Points* using the same method as for analysing advertisements.

ALWAYS MAKE A ROUGH DRAFT

Each and every time, photocopy the form and put the original in a file, clean and flat. This important advice is often ignored. That is why many good candidates spoil their chances by sending in forms with a poor layout and littered with crossings out or white correction fluid. Nothing looks more slipshod. High standards of presentation are as important as with your CV and self-marketing letters. Make all of your mistakes on the rough draft, and only copy it to the actual form when you are happy with your answers.

CAREFULLY READ THE APPLICATION FORM

AND ANY ACCOMPANYING MATERIAL

Look for any instructions on how to complete the form (sometimes they are found on the rear page). Most candidates don't give these forms the care and time they need. This gives the diligent and painstaking applicant a better than average chance, of course. Remember that, as far as you are concerned, the sole purpose is to get an interview.

A frequent requirement is that black ink or a black ball-point is used. Some demand that you use only your own handwriting. Others allow a typed or word-processed response, and this can be particularly effective for an administrative, secretarial or IT job, striking familiar chords and demonstrating ability with the equipment.

Check to see if accompanying CVs and letters are permitted – some employers (e.g. a few local authorities) specifically debar them on the grounds of equal opportunities policies.

FILL IN THE MUNDANE FACTUAL INFORMATION

If you did your earlier preparation correctly, this should be is fairly straightforward as you have already listed the dates and much of the information that you require. However, you should still use your rough copy to enter details such as your name, address, date of birth, employment record, qualifications and so on. Apart from anything else, you can gauge how large your handwriting has to be to fit everything onto the form. Obey all instructions and do not leave blank spaces. Where a particular question is irrelevant put 'N/A' (which stands for 'Not Applicable'). Work your way through the form, carefully responding to each question.

AVOID NEGATIVE FEATURES

Keep negative points off the application form as they spoil your chances. It is, however, a legal document and any untruths could provide grounds for dismissal if discovered. Conversely, it isn't a confessional box which requires you to parade your sins and omissions.

If you see redundancy as an opportunity to broaden your experience, which it is, then say so. Note, however, that it is always the job and not the person that is redundant. As a general rule, always give a positive rather than a negative reason for leaving a job, e.g. 'self-advancement' or 'increased responsibility'. Certainly never hint at strife or individual problems.

TAKE CARE WHEN GIVING YOUR SALARY DETAILS

Many application forms ask for details about your salary in previous jobs. There are obvious potential problems for you in this: if your salary was low it can demean your worth to the prospective employer and you may not even get an interview; on the other hand, you risk deterring the recruiter if the figure is too high.

The best advice is to consider the estimated financial value of the job in relation to your present/last position. For example, you may consider that the job for which you are applying carries a likely salary of £18 to £20,000, while your most recent position had a salary of £15,000 plus overtime, BUPA and other allowances. If you simply put down '£15,000' it would be incorrect, as it is probably worth a good deal more than that. In these circumstances it is reasonable to write '£18,000 with benefits and bonus'. This is usefully ambiguous because it isn't clear if the figure already includes benefits or if it's a baseline. You can be clarify this at an interview if necessary.

COMPLETING THE 'FREE RESPONSE' SECTION

This is the part that is variously headed 'State your reasons for applying for this position', or perhaps, 'Provide other information in support of your application'. There is often a large space, with an invitation to use additional sheets if necessary. Many applicants half-heartedly scribble a few lines. Some even leave it blank altogether, or simply write 'See CV'. This is a major mistake because interviews are won and lost in this section of an application form. In fact, you should treat this is an invitation to tell the recruiter all the reasons why you should be interviewed and, indeed, why you should be offered the job. Most importantly, it is a major platform for you to parade your *Prime Selling Points*.

You should spend some time drafting your statement using the following structure and subheadings:

1. Short opening statement and introduction

2. Work experience

3. Relevant skills and attributes

4. Qualifications and Training

5. Summary

The very fact that you use a carefully structured and logical approach will immediately set you apart from most of the other applicants. The sections below deal with each of the subheadings in turn.

Opening statement

Use a sharp opening statement which tells the recruiter how you intend to tackle the task in hand, demonstrating a methodical and planned approach:

> *My proven skills and experience would, I feel, enable me to make a significant contribution in this role. In support of my application, this section is structured as follows:*
>
> *1. Work experience*
> *2. Qualifications and training*
> *3. Personal qualities*

Work experience

Under this heading briefly refer to other workplaces and experience that have relevance to this particular application. For example:

> *My experience with Foster Brothers includes several vital aspects of this role, including…*
>
> *I received an excellent grounding in this area with Brown Brothers, where I was a successful Team Leader for six years.*

Relevant skills and attributes

Commence this section by stating:

> *I can demonstrate extensive experience which includes the major requirements for this role. In particular I would emphasise the following: …*

Now construct short paragraphs and sentences which outline each of your *Prime Selling Points* for this job. List them in a bullet-point format, ideally providing some supporting evidence:

- *Excellent administrative skills. Received comprehensive training in all aspects, successfully running the day-to-day activities of a busy office.*

- *Computer-literate with extensive experience in using Microsoft Office. Produced a range of presentation materials for Amarex sales representatives, using Powerpoint.*

- *Excellent customer relations skills, with proven ability in dealing with sensitive situations while maintaining confidentiality.*

List each of your *Prime Selling Points* in this way. Note that it does not hurt to cover the same points twice, using different words. For example, if there is a major requirement for excellent communication skills, you can list it with an illustrative example in your work experience and you can also make the point when describing your personal attributes.

Once you have covered your *Prime Selling Points*, carefully check the job description and advertisement again and construct similar bullet points that demonstrate your ability to satisfy each of the remaining requirements that are mentioned. Try to make sure that every single point is covered. Do not be shy about stating your skills and attributes in a positive manner.

Particularly relevant qualifications and training

Make a point of highlighting relevant training in this part of any application form, even if it is already listed elsewhere:

In addition to formal educational qualifications, I have successfully completed a number of intensive Customer Care courses. I am currently completing a distance learning course in counselling.

If you have no training courses or qualifications that are worth listing, then it is best to omit this heading from the free response section.

Write a short concluding paragraph

This is a chance to draw all the threads together and emphasise your enthusiasm for the job. It all shows that you have a logical and rational mind, providing a beginning, a middle and an end.

Use a separate sheet of good quality A4 writing paper if required.

COMPLETING YOUR APPLICATION

If unsure of your grammar, punctuation or spelling, ask a trusted friend or relative to check it for you. When satisfied, carefully copy your answers onto the original copy. Then:

1. Write a self-marketing letter to accompany the application form, again emphasising your *Prime Selling Points*. A brief couple of lines simply will not do! Write your letter in the same manner as if you were only supplying a CV rather than an application form. The worst that can happen is that it will be discarded – on the other hand, it might tip the balance in your favour.

2. Tailor your CV to highlight the *Prime Selling Points* for this position.

3. Photocopy the completed application form and keep it in your files, along with the job description, advertisement, your analysis sheet, self-marketing letter, targeted CV and any other relevant paperwork.

4. Despatch the letter, application form and CV, *attached together with a paper clip and unfolded*, in a plain A4 envelope. If you have a manager's name, then endorse the envelope 'Confidential' (which should ensure that your application then reaches the person directly and gains early, hopefully favourable, attention).

This is a painstaking and thorough approach that takes some time but it is infinitely more likely to succeed than a half-hearted and hurried effort. Once you have completed one form in this way, you will find that much of the information will be useful for other applications.

Chapter 16

Making speculative approaches

CANVASSING FOR JOB VACANCIES THAT HAVE NOT BEEN ADVERTISED IS A VERY SUC-
CESSFUL JOB HUNTING METHOD AND THIS CHAPTER SHOWS YOU HOW TO DO IT
EFFECTIVELY.

This area of job-search can be broadly divided into two separate activities:

■ speculative letters;

■ telephone approaches.

This chapter covers both topics because they are successful job-hunting methods that
trawl the hidden job markets and uncover opportunities that would otherwise be
missed. Many people are loathe to try these 'cold calling' techniques because of the
likelihood of rejection. This, however, is an inherent and necessary part of using
these techniques. Nobody likes rejection, and almost everyone dislikes making 'cold'
telephone approaches, but remember that every successful job getting campaign
takes the following pattern:

No, No, No, No, No, No, No, No... YES

Furthermore, you are in command of your own career. You can disconnect the telephone call or throw letters into the waste bin at any time. Also, you are aiming for
an incredibly low success rate. One good answer is all that you need!

MOUNTING A SPECULATIVE LETTER CAMPAIGN

In addition to the ongoing turnover of job applications in response to advertisements, you should also aim to send out regular batches of direct approach letters
each week. Rather than waiting for employers to advertise, you approach them
directly and ask if there are any suitable vacancies.

Aim for at least 15 letters each week! This is a heavy enough workload because it
involves both producing the letters and following them up at a later date. This

method is worth the cost in time and postage as it has proved a particularly effective job-getting method.

The addresses are obtained from your own employer database, compiled by researching your chosen job markets. The basic techniques are similar to those used in replying to advertisements, although it is necessary to use a 'broad brush' when targeting your job-getting documents.

The first task is to decide upon four or five *Prime Selling Points* that you feel will gain the most resonance from recruiters in the job market. With no advertisement to analyse, you will have to make an informed guess. This becomes quite easy to do with some practice. However, if you need help, it is a good idea to monitor advertisements to see what most employers currently need.

The first task is to produce a CV targeted towards each of your chosen job markets. Use the same method of editing your library resource CV, as described earlier in this book:

1. Incorporate your *Prime Selling Points* on the front page.

2. Rewrite your personal profile.

3. Suitably amend job titles to reflect the context of the skills and experience that you are marketing.

This time, of course, you are aiming at more general job requirements, because it is unwise to limit yourself to specific types of job within your profession, trade or chosen work. Nevertheless, when you have responded to a few job advertisements, you will probably find that one of your targeted CVs can be easily amended

WRITING SPECULATIVE SELF-MARKETING LETTERS

A similar technique is used, again relying upon bulleted *Prime Selling Points*. The difference, however, is that the very same letter is sent, separately addressed, to different employers in your chosen sector. You can usefully slightly amend some letters if you want to refer to a recent newspaper report regarding the company, for example; little tricks like this personalise your letters. Remember to always write to named line managers – not 'Personnel' or 'Dear Sir or Madam'.

For this purpose, you do not use a heading and the style of the 'Tempter' paragraph has to be amended slightly. The following opening is a reasonable example:

As a very experienced IT professional with an excellent career record achieved within major organisations, I feel that my skills will be of value to your company. The enclosed CV details my career history and skills, and the following points may be particularly relevant: ...

Note that the person is described as an 'IT professional' rather than adopting a specific job title. After all, there may be many different computer-related jobs within the company, and some might be worth considering. This opening paragraph implicitly invites the reader both to read the letter and study the CV.

The final 'Action' paragraph is very straight forward. Consider the things that you want to happen as a result of the letter: an interview or meeting, perhaps a telephone discussion. The ending almost writes itself:

> *I would welcome the opportunity of a meeting to discuss how I might meet your company's needs, and would appreciate any advice or assistance that you can offer. I trust that you will not object if I telephone within the next week to progress my enquiry.*

All that remains is to insert the bulleted *Prime Selling Points* and add the addresses.

Repeat this procedure for each of your chosen job markets: a separate targeted CV and letter for each sector. This task needs to be done only once (although you may later wish to amend your documents in the light of ensuing feedback).

KEEPING A JOB-SEARCH LOG

Besides making a note on your employer database sheet, make sure that you keep accurate records of all speculative approaches in your job-search log. This is an important administrative feature of any major project. There is simply too much happening in an effective job-getting campaign to rely on memory alone. Besides which, you need to maintain a schedule of follow-up calls: after sending out a speculative direct approach, you will telephone the manager and continue the self-marketing exercise. It also helps to keep track of your various activities.

USING THE TELEPHONE IN YOUR JOB-SEARCH

The telephone is an important and often underrated tool in your job search armoury. Indeed, in this age of instant communication many employers tend to use the telephone to contact candidates rather than traditional letters.

> Always make sure that your job-search files is located near to the telephone so that you will not be caught unawares if an employer rings regarding one of your applications.

Employers also accept that many people will use the telephone to canvas them about potential job vacancies. From the job-hunter's point of view, this is a very efficient and productive method, both in terms of time and results. It is the most personal approach other than a face-to-face meeting. Besides which, it is just one more step in the PSP system, which leaves no job-getting avenue unexplored. It is also accepted that sometimes, no matter how beautifully your letters and CVs are produced, they might be unread in a busy office and simply thrown away.

There are a number of distinct advantages in using the telephone to contact likely employers. With a telephone approach you can:

- contact more employers and follow up more leads, increasing your chances of finding suitable vacancies;

- find unadvertised vacancies and make instantaneous applications, beating the competition;

- work from the comfort of your own home or office, with ready access to your job-hunting materials;

- usually get an immediate answer instead of waiting for a reply to a letter;

- develop the conversation according to the employer's responses;

- get across your personality and enthusiasm;

- identify the employer's needs and enquire about more than one type of job;

- ask about other companies which may have vacancies;

- arrange to call in for a chat.

Many people are unduly apprehensive about using this 'cold canvas' method, but nerves can be overcome with a planned approach to making telephone calls. It is the same principle as used by trained telesales staff who *always* have a carefully worded script. As with any method of job getting, preparation is vital in making a telephone call really work for you.

Preparation

Using your employer database, make a telephone contact list of potential employers in each job market. You can use your main contact log for this and keep your activity record up-to-date at the same time.

It is necessary to find the correct name of the appropriate line manager: the person who you would expect to head the department in which you want to work. Names quoted in reference books quickly become dated, even at director level – the latest issue may be a year old, and some people will inevitably have moved on. With instant telephone communication you need up-to-date information. This is also the case when writing to the company – incorrectly addressed letters *may* get passed on, but it is best to avoid the risk.

It is much better to telephone the company on the previous day. Telephonists, receptionists and secretaries have the undeserved reputation of trying to thwart all incoming calls from job-seekers when, in fact, they can be very helpful. It all depends upon the questions you ask and how you ask them:

> *Good morning/afternoon, I am writing a letter to your Works Manager/Maintenance Manager/Quality Control Manager … What is the name and formal job title please…*

> **Position a mirror near to your telephone and smile into it as you speak: it will make you sound friendly and interested. Try it!**

It is important to adopt an authoritative and assertive tone (not bombastic) and *expect* an answer to your polite instruction. You will find that the information is usually given without hesitation. On the other hand, if you sound diffident or unsure of yourself, it gives the impression that you feel that you have no right to the information and you aren't likely to get it. So be positive and confident, as if routinely telephoning from the office of another company on a business matter. It is best to use non-gender language: referring to 'him' when it should be 'her' can be counter-productive.

If the telephonist asks the nature of your business, say that it is confidential. On the rare occasions when the person who answers the telephone does not give you the details, then ask for the Sales Department and try again. Only as a last resort should you try the Personnel Department (staff there tend to be experts in deflecting job enquiries which make more work for them).

You have presumably already done your homework on the company in your job research, but make sure that you know something about the company before ringing.

Planning a script

It is good practice to have a clear plan on paper of who you are going to telephone, the purpose of your call and what you are going to say. This will help you to keep to the point.

> **When telephoning a company, always keep your objective to get a face-to-face meeting clearly in mind.**

Prepare a brief but interesting general introduction. Keep to the point but be friendly. Practise your introduction aloud until you are satisfied. Use sentences that do not invite a 'yes' or 'no' answer: if the answer is a direct 'no' the conversation is ended. Instead, say that you are reviewing your career options and would welcome any advice or assistance. This gives you the chance to tell the manager something about yourself.

Rehearse the script aloud, either to yourself or with a partner (if you can ignore the inevitable leg-pulling). It is a good idea to ring a trusted friend or relative and rehearse the opening to see how it comes across on the telephone.

Making the call

When you have completed the initial preparation you should:

- ensure that your CV *for the specific job market* is in front of you as an extra script and aide-mémoire;

- decide the best time to telephone, usually sticking to standard office hours and avoiding lunchtimes;

- ask for the line manager by name;

- speak clearly and confidently: use a pleasant but authoritative tone when speaking to the person who first answers your call – give the clear impression that you expect to be put through.

Passing the guard

It is not always easy to reach the right person. In fact there is usually a 'guard' positioned between you and the line manager, and this person will usually be skilled at screening incoming calls. *Do not tell this person why you are calling.* Say that you are following up on recent confidential correspondence.

If you cannot reach your target manager, do not use your presentation on another, more junior person. This is invariably a waste of time and may ruin the whole initiative. You can too often receive a terse 'No' from someone who has no authority to hire you anyway.

Give the confident impression that the line manager will want to speak to you. If this fails, do not try to browbeat the person or become bombastic. If offered to be put through to someone else, decline politely. Simply ask when it might be convenient to call again. As a last resort, you may find that calling near lunchtime or towards the end of the working day might catch the guard off-station.

Speaking to the line manager

Be friendly but formal. Introduce yourself using the prepared introduction. Thereafter, use your script as a prompt, not as an indispensable crutch. Vary your tone of voice – dull monotones are a giveway that a script is being used. Try to talk at medium levels of pace and volume.

Obviously, any conversation is a two-way communication, and you must allow the manager to respond without interrupting. Be alert for clues as to the employer's current needs. Try to develop the conversation, telling him or her what you can offer, using your CV and script as a prompt. Be business-like and efficient, confining your discussion to relevant points.

Your conversation should include the following points:

- Ask if you can deliver your CV in person and perhaps have a face-to-face chat. Failing that, ask if you can mail your CV and enquire if a company application form can be sent to you.

- If the employer has no immediate vacancies, ask how you can get on their prospect list for future vacancies. Does he know of any other firms with vacancies?

- At the end of the call, summarise any agreed action, e.g. you will send your CV, or phone back next week, and so on.

- Thank the manager for his or her time. Always end positively and politely, even if the answer is 'no'.

Be persistent!

When you begin a canvassing campaign such as this, you know that you will receive rejections. That is the whole nature of the exercise: you are simply searching through the 'Noes' to find the glittering 'Ayes'. Remember that a rejection is not a personal insult: paradoxically, it is an everyday part of job-getting. Above all, don't give up. Persistence rather than genius is the real key to success. (There are plenty of failed geniuses, whereas few really dogged triers are unsuccessful!)

Some don'ts

- Don't get demoralised by rejections or put off if you receive an offhand response (you probably would not want to work with a person like that, anyway). Most people will be helpful and pleasant.

- Don't simply pick up the telephone and ask the first person who answers, 'Have you got any jobs?'

- Don't address the manager by his or her first name unless invited to do so.

- Don't invite 'no' answers by asking directly if there are any vacancies – better to say that you are reviewing your career options and would welcome any help and advice.

- Don't prolong the call with unnecessary and irrelevant chatter.

CHECKLIST FOR SPECULATIVE TELEPHONE

CALLS TO AN EMPLOYER

You will need:

▪ your CV prepared for the specific job market;

▪ your employer database file and spare blank sheets;

▪ your contact log;

▪ a notepad and pen;

▪ a prepared introduction, giving some initial information about your relevant skills and experience.

Your procedure:

1. Make a list of companies to be contacted using your contact log.

2. Prepare a page for each employer in your employer database file. (Make a preliminary call to obtain the name and title of the appropriate line manager.)

3. Make the call and ask for the line manager (head of department).

4. Introduce yourself using your prepared introduction.

5. Ask for a meeting to discuss possible openings and to explore how you might meet the company's needs.

6. Repeat any agreed courses of action.

7. Thank the manager for his or her time, ending positively and politely.

Chapter 17 ∎

Conducting job-getting meetings

BECOME A SUCCESSFUL INTERVIEW CANDIDATE BY USING THE TECHNIQUES DESCRIBED IN THIS CHAPTER.

PREPARING FOR THE INTERVIEW

It will be apparent by now that the PSP system leaves nothing to chance. This is especially so when it comes to attending interviews. The more thorough your preparation, then the more effective your presentation will be. Read the invitation letter carefully. Check the day and time of the meeting, and where it is to take place; make an entry in your diary and do not rely on your memory. Note whether or not you are required to confirm your attendance.

Ask yourself the following questions:

■ Who is going to interview you?

■ What kind of interview will it be?

■ Will you be expected to do any tests and, if so, what tests will they be?

■ Is there a job specification or outline, and do you have it?

If you do not know the answer to any of these questions, you should telephone the writer and ask for clarification. If practicable, it is a good idea to do a practice journey at the time of day your interview is to take place to check transport, traffic and parking.

RESEARCHING THE COMPANY

It is important that you find out everything you can about the company. This may include:

■ names of company chairman, directors and so on;

■ products and services;

- details of how the company developed;

- markets;

- turnover;

- profit;

- plans for the future;

- number of branches/sites;

- number of people employed;

- company philosophy;

- types of equipment used.

Your employer database and job vacancy sheet will contain some useful details, but you should also take steps to obtain as much information as possible.

> Buy a small notebook to take with you to interviews. Write down your *Prime Selling Points*, questions to ask and so on. Recruiters regard this as acceptable, and it indicates a methodical and efficient approach.

You should also seek to find information about the industry, particularly if you have not worked in this before. It is very poor form for a candidate to turn up to an interview knowing little about the job, the organisation or the industry.

Where to find information

You will find valuable information by consulting the large business directories at any large library:

- *Key British Enterprises*

- *Kompass* – UK and Ireland

- *Kelly's Business Directory*

- *Personnel Managers Year Book*

- *The Stock Exchange Official Year Book*

- *The Financial Times Top 1000*

- *Who Owns Whom*

- *Directory of Directors*

- *Macmillan Unquoted Companies*

Business Information Service – British Library, London

You can also use the Business Information Service (BIS), which is part of the British Library in London. The BIS has a massive collection of business information literature. This includes market research reports and journals, directories, company annual reports, trade and business journals and house journals and trade literature. There is also a CD-ROM service for personal callers. The opening hours are Monday to Friday 09.30 – 20.00 and Saturday 10.00 – 13.00.

Anyone can use the BIS Reading Room, free of charge, and there is no formal admission procedure. You will simply be asked to sign the visitors' book. Staff will help you to find the most appropriate sources to start your research.

Company literature

Many companies and organisations produce publicity leaflets, either for the business as a whole or for their products. This can be easily obtained by telephoning and asking for it to be sent to you. It is not necessary to deal with the personnel department when making your contact, although doing so may impress them that you are doing your homework. Company annual reports offer a wealth of information and can be obtained on request.

Internet and CD-Roms

This is a potent source of information, and many companies have their own websites. Simply use one of the Internet search engines (see Chapter 7) and enter the company name in the dialogue box. You will probably be surprised at the things that are offered. Print the relevant pages and study them at your leisure rather than using costly telecommunications time.

Many libraries carry CD-Roms that contain news reports from UK newspapers. It is worth checking if there have been any reports about the company that you are interested in. Recent knowledge of this type can suitably impress a recruiter.

REVIEW THE JOB APPLICATION

If you have a job specification, then read it carefully again. Are there any new points that were not apparent in the advertisement and which were not covered in your original application? Go through each point and tick off the requirements that you meet, and note potential areas of weakness (do not be unduly daunted by them – you have been selected for an interview, after all).

Talk to someone who knows about the job, even if this means telephoning the company to which you are applying. At worst, this will demonstrate a methodical approach and initiative.

Finally, review your employment database notes, and reread the original advertisement. Decide if anything has changed or if any new information has emerged to change your initial strategy.

Decide on your *Prime Selling Points*

In the light of the recently researched information, read through the CV, self-marketing letter and, if applicable, the application form that you submitted for this job. Consider again which of your attributes best match the job *Key Competencies Required*. In the absence of better information, stick with the original bulleted *Prime Selling Points*. These are the points that have won you the interview. They will represent your main agenda at the interview. Recruiters find this consistency very reassuring. Do not be too ready to discard any element of your existing strategy and remember that it has got you this far.

Make sure that you note your selected *Prime Selling Points* in your notebook.

It is a good idea to prepare and practise answers to a few anticipated questions, learning the skills of deftly turning the point to illustrate a *Prime Selling Point*. Most politicians are particularly adept at this method of getting across their predetermined points, and you should approach the interview with the same objective.

Possible 'negatives'

There are both positive and negative aspects to any interviewer's tactics. The first will explore your strengths to see why you should be given the job, while the second will probe your weaknesses to see why you shouldn't be employed. The more precious interview time that is taken up with negative interviewing, then the less chance to sell your *Prime Selling Points*.

That is why the PSP system stresses the need to ensure against such negatives being built into your job application (and thus avoid a common fault of many unsuccessful job-seekers). However, if you are aware of any important omissions or deficiencies, then you should anticipate any awkward questions.

The strategy is to quickly satisfy the recruiter's doubts, but also to immediately direct the interview to a *Prime Selling Point*. The tactics are to devise suitable responses beforehand in case the questions are asked.

You should then practise your answers aloud, either to a mirror or with a friend who can play the 'devil's advocate'. Thinking about your the answer is one thing, but the spoken word is sometimes a different thing altogether. This could be a vital turning-point of the interview, and you need to find a form of words that is both effective and natural to you.

The words do not always come out as we intend them and practice will enable you to sell yourself in a way that is comfortable and natural.

Your questions

'Do you have any questions for us?'

It is surprising how many people answer, 'No, I think you've covered them.' This creates exactly the wrong impression and wastes further opportunities to push your *Prime Selling Points*. Always prepare four or five questions of your own; this number should mean that some will inevitably still be relevant at the end of an interview. They should arise from your research into the company and its activities, and also strongly connect with your *Prime Selling Points*:

> *'I see that you intend to expand into electronic alarms systems. As I have a lot of experience in positioning new products in the market, I wonder if you could explain what the company plans to do in that respect.'*

Your questions can concern future training, technical matters, sales and marketing, new products...anything that demonstrates your interest and illustrates a *Prime Selling Point*.

One powerful technique is to use the invitation to ask questions as an opportunity to recap your *Prime Selling Points*, and then ask the interviewer how he or she sees them being used in the organisation. To answer the question, the interviewer has to imagine you being part of the company and already doing the job.

Write your questions in your notebook. Do not include questions about salary, sick schemes, pensions, holidays and other benefits. Treat the interview purely as a means of selling your skills and experience. Besides, you are in a much stronger bargaining position when the recruiters decide that they want you for the job. That is when you have successfully sold what you have to offer, which is necessary before you can really put a price on it.

An opening statement

'Tell me something about yourself.'

This is a very common opening to an interview. The invitation often comes within seconds of a candidate's arrival in the interview room. It too often catches the person unawares and brings a muffled, waffling response. This usually sets the tone for a bad interview! Yet it is a wonderful opportunity for the well-prepared job-getter to outline his or her *Prime Selling Points* and set the scene for a very focused and successful interview.

You therefore need to write a two-minute 'commercial' that embodies each of your chosen PSPs. Do not include inconsequential details, such as hobbies or family interests. Keep your message to the point. Practise it aloud until it rolls off your tongue. Smile into the mirror while you are saying it. Rehearse the statement in the car when you are driving to the interview.

Your time will not be wasted, even if the question is not asked. The much-practised statement will also provide a very useful aide-mémoire that lists your *Prime Selling Points*.

Strengths

'What is your greatest strength?'

This is another popular, almost inevitable question. It may come in a variety of other guises, such as 'What do you feel you can bring to this organisation?' or 'What would your previous boss say about your strengths?'

Using the PSP system, the answer is obvious. As far as this interview is concerned, your greatest strengths (note the plural) are the four or five *Prime Selling Points*. Give your answer without hesitation, listing one PSP after the other, even if you have only been asked to give one strength. If asked to prioritise your list, then give the PSP which you adjudge to be the most important for the job, regardless of whether that really is your greatest strength.

'What is your greatest weakness?'

If asked about strengths, then this question will follow as surely as night follows day. Many applicants dread the question. Some even answer it truthfully! Let's be clear that it is no part of your responsibility as a candidate to parade your weaknesses. Your task is to be positive and present the best case for your skills and experiences.

So when you answer this question, provide one or more of your *Prime Selling Points* cunningly wrapped in a supposed weakness:

> 'Well, we must all have faults and I'm no exception, but I am committed to continuous improvement. I try to respond positively to constructive criticism and do something about any weaknesses that are identified. One recent example was when a colleague made me aware that I needed to improve my knowledge of creating websites to give me the skills needed to monitor the consultants who were providing our website maintenance. I took a course on this and practised my skills until it's now one of my greatest assets.'

An answer such as this demonstrates a number of strengths: you respond to positive criticism, you quickly learn new skills, you are constantly aiming for high standards… It does not even begin to offer a weakness.

The important thing is to have this answer worked out in advance.

Leaving statement

It is also a good idea to know when and how to 'get off the stage'. Prepare a friendly but business-like parting statement:

'Thank you for your time and courtesy. I've enjoyed the interview and feel that it's been useful. It certainly has increased both my interest in the job, and my ability to be of value.'

Visualise gathering your belongings, rising with a smile, giving a firm handshake and leaving the room with some style. This may make you feel silly but it is better than falling over your briefcase at the actual interview

'BEFORE THE INTERVIEW' CHECKLIST

Have you:

- Established your *Prime Selling Points*?

- Conducted extensive research to find information about the job, the organisation and the industry?

- Prepared four or five of your own questions arising from your research?

- Prepared and practised a two-minute opening statement?

- Identified any potential deficiencies and formulated suitable responses to likely questions about them?

- Prepared and practised an answer to the question 'What is your greatest strength?' Your answer, again, will list the *Prime Selling Points*.

- Prepared and practised an answer to the question 'What is your greatest weakness?'

- Prepared and practised a parting statement?

- Carefully read the letter of invitation to interview?

- Confirmed your intention to attend?

- Found out who is going to interview you?

- Got details of the format and likely duration of the interview?

- Checked if there will be any any tests?

- Made suitable travel arrangements?

- Organised your personal presentation and hygiene?

- Prepared suitable, clean and pressed clothing?

- Talked to anyone doing a similar job?

- Read through the CV, self-marketing letter and application form?

- Made notes of key points?

ATTENDING THE INTERVIEW

The time has come for the meeting and you are probably better prepared than any other candidate. This should be reason enough for confidence. Also, of course, you have your own agenda and a list of *Prime Selling Points* that you are bringing to the market.

It is best to allow plenty of time to get there to avoid arriving flustered and breathless or, worse still, late. If you are too early, you can either find a café or sit in your car and read through your notes.

Arriving

When you have found the building, do not enter too early. You will only get in the way and idle time will give your 'internal chatterbox' a time to persuade you that you won't get the job. Aim to be about 10 minutes early. Visit the cloakroom, comb your hair and check your appearance in the mirror.

Please remember to be polite and friendly to the reception staff. It is easy to forget this if you are feeling nervous. Besides being a common courtesy, remember that these people are already in the team you aspire to join and they are often asked for their opinions about candidates. Be polite and friendly but never flirtatious. Ask to leave your briefcase and outer coat at reception, having removed your papers to a smart folder.

Spend any time that is available reading any house journals, trade magazines or promotional literature that is offered. Watch others and get a feel for the culture by seeing how people are behaving. You should also recall your *Prime Selling Points* by inwardly reciting your prepared opening statement.

Views differ, but it is probably best to politely decline if offered tea or coffee. It is something to go wrong: a spilled drink over the recruiter's trousers will not win you any friends. Besides which, if you are nervous, it can be loudly signalled by the cup rattling on the saucer. You should certainly decline the offer of a cigarette.

Entering the meeting room

Momentarily before entering the room, when passing through the door, consciously pull back your shoulders and draw yourself to your full height. Do not worry if this is seen by the recruiter – in fact that's the general idea. It shows that you are setting out to do justice both to yourself and to the interviewer.

Smile confidently as you walk in, making eye contact but not to the exclusion of all else in the room. It is natural to glance around as you enter any unknown area – part of our instinctive and inherited behaviour. It is usually an unconscious act and its absence will strike a similarly unconscious warning in the interviewer.

Introduce yourself and greet the interviewer by name, but do not use his or her first name unless specifically asked to do so. Exchange a brief, firm and dry handshake (wipe your hands before entering if nervous and moist-palmed).

Sitting

Do not sit until invited to do so, and then sit well back in the seat with both feet firmly grounded on the floor. Move the chair to the side as you sit so that you are slightly side-on to the interviewer; this avoids a face to face confrontation. Do not fold your arms. Sit upright in your chair in a relaxed manner. This position enables you to lean forward to demonstrate interest, or lean back in thought. Maintain eye contact and look calmly at the interviewer.

Take your CV from your folder and ask the interviewer if he or she minds if you take notes. Don't put your papers on the recruiter's desk. Avoid fidgeting or fiddling with your pen.

The meeting

Silence is a technique used by some interviewers: they are interested to see how you respond. So wait for the interviewer to commence the proceedings and on no account should you nervously blurt out your opening statement to fill the vacuum.

Remember that your objective is to get an offer of the job. You are going to achieve this by focusing sharply on your *Prime Selling Points*.

Gain the interviewer's confidence by listening attentively as he or she explains the job and talks about the company. Look for additional clues about the emloyer's needs. Do not talk unnecessarily. Again, beware of the calculated silence that can lead a candidate to think that more is needed when, in fact, a satisfactory answer has been given; in such circumstances a person can unwittingly reveal all sorts of things.

Be Alert to push your *Prime Selling Points*

Many interviewers talk too much, particularly at the beginning and end of a meeting. Indeed, poor interviewers tend to monopolise the time. You need to be patient and don't interrupt but be alert for opportunities to sell your *Prime Selling Points*.

Push your *Prime Selling Points*

When invited to talk about yourself, parade your *Prime Selling Points* to demonstrate how you will provide the employer with benefits. Inevitably, when selling a limited number of points, there will be some duplication. Do not be concerned about this, although you should obviously try to find different ways of highlighting these main strengths and achievements related to the job. Remember that recruiters prefer a confident and assured candidate.

Don't raise negatives – push your *Prime Selling Points*

Although you have prepared answers to questions regarding your negatives, never raise the issue yourself. Even if you handle it well, negative statements always attract more follow-up questions and waste interview time. Many people who think they have had an excellent interview have, in fact, spent most of their time talking about negatives. So keep positive!

Display a cheerful, open personality with a ready smile. Talk freely and vary the tone of your voice as you do in normal conversation. Jokes can be misplaced. An interview meeting is serious business and, anyway, the interviewer's sense of humour may be different from yours.

Avoid criticising former employers – it makes a negative statement about your loyalty and your relationship with authority. However, be ready to defend your own views in a constructive but non-combative manner. Do not argue, even if you strongly disagree with the interviewer's views.

Keep pushing your *Prime Selling Points*

By allowing the interviewer to concentrate on the main issues of the job, you also allow yourself to focus your answers on your *Prime Selling Points*. Try to turn every question to demonstrate one of the these highly marketable assets. Explain the benefits they will bring the company.

Take the opportunity to ask questions during the interview, if this is possible. This turns the interview into a discussion. However, save a couple of your prepared questions for the end of the meeting when you will be invited to ask them.

Do not ask about terms of employment at this interview. Try to avoid the matter until later. If it is inescapable, then always allow the interviewer to state the employer's terms first. Instead of immediately responding with your bargaining position, reserve your case and say that you would like time to think about it.

Finally, don't forget to push your *Prime Selling Points*

Use any late opportunity to reiterate your *Prime Selling Points*, if possible leaving a vivid impression in the recruiter's mind. Then, when the interview is signalled as being over, end with your prepared parting statement of your suitability for the job. Thank the interviewer, shake hands again, and leave with a smile.

AFTER THE MEETING

A positive benefit of using a focused agenda is that you can accurately assess your performance. Your objective was to sell the selected *Prime Selling Points*. How successful were you? How did you feel that the interview went? It is important to analyse and note your feelings while everything is still fresh in your mind but probably after the adrenalin has stopped pumping. Complete an interview record sheet and keep it in your file for future reference.

You should also consider the effectiveness of your *Prime Selling Points*. Which of them interested the recruiter? Note any questions where you experienced difficulty, and any areas where you felt that you failed. (This may be your perception rather than that of the recruiter, of course.)

More importantly, take note of possible learning outcomes:

- How can you market your *Prime Selling Points* more effectively?
- How much of the interview concerned positives and how much time was spent on negatives?
- Did you talk too much or too little?
- Was your preparation correct and can it be improved?
- Were your questions well received?
- Did you arrive on time?
- Were you suitably dressed and groomed?
- Were you enthusiastic enough?
- Do you need to listen more to the interviewer's questions?
- How could you improve your performance next time?

Remember that other candidates are in the field and you have no idea of their qualities. Do not be unduly depressed by a rejection, even when you felt that the interview went well. You cannot lose by attending a job-getting meeting: at the very least you will have added to your experience.

You will find that you get better at interviews with practice. In fact, after a short time in your campaign, you will probably have more recent interview experience than the recruiters. Be persistent. Search for continual improvement in your techniques, and continue to have faith in your *Prime Selling Points*. The PSP system will inevitably produce the results you need. Believe in yourself and believe in PSP!

NEGOTIATING TERMS AND CONDITIONS

The ultimate aim of the PSP job-getting system is to win the next job that is right for you. Inevitably you will get job offers. The ideal situation is to get more than one offer, so that you have a real choice.

How will you choose the right job? Sometimes, of course, the answer will be self-evident. Do remember that finance is not the only consideration.

However, the question of remuneration has to be addressed and assessed. Salary and terms are often negotiable. The optimum salary will depend upon the value placed on your skills and attributes by the employer. Whether you actually achieve that optimum salary, however, may depend on your negotiating skills

> Be prepared to negotiate as a free and equal party. Remember that the employer has already decided that you are the person the organisation needs.

You should have a clear idea of the minimum terms of employment you would be prepared to accept. Make a realistic assessment of your required income. On no account accept less than this, only to regret it later. Do not offer your services at a discount – other employers will pay for quality. A better offer will come your way – believe it!

Of course, much depends on whether you already have a job. It has to be admitted that even the worst offer is usually better value than Jobseekers Allowance.

If you do have a current job, then compare the salary, conditions, prospects and benefits that are offered by the position. Consider the whole package and do not fall into the trap of comparing 'apples with oranges'. Try to asses the value of any perks, such as a company car or health scheme. What is your current *net* monthly salary and what will the alternative job offer? Will you be losing money by changing your job, and is it a justifiable loss?

If the job involves the relocation of your home, how does this affect the rest of your family? Will the company pay relocation costs? In these circumstances, you also need to consider differences in the cost of living and in property prices.

Negotiating terms

Begin by asking the employer to make an opening offer. You should then table a number of questions:

■ Does this salary fit into a collective bargaining pay structure?

If the answer to this question is 'Yes', then there is probably little chance of changing the offer. However, it allows the security of regular pay reviews in solidarity with your colleagues.

■ How is the annual salary made up – how much is basic salary and what other elements does it include (bonuses, etc.)?

■ When would the salary be reviewed?

■ What performance and payment indicators will be used?

Be careful of fudged or hazy responses. 'You can be sure we'll look after you' is no kind of promise at all.

Other important may questions include:

■ Will any vocational training be provided and what is its value?

■ Is there a pension and when will you become eligible to participate?

■ Is there an employee share-saving or profit-sharing scheme and, if so, what kind is it and when will you become eligible to participate?

■ Will you be given a company car? If not, will the company pay expenses for the use of your own vehicle? At what rate (pence per mile)?

■ If you intend to commute by rail, will the employer pay or help with the costs? Will it provide a an interest-free season ticket loan, for example?

■ Will the employer provide private health insurance, and when will you beome eligible to join? Is it non-contributory?

These perks can be worth a considerable amount of money over the year. However, the Inland Revenue are well aware of this and will charge you accordingly!

Finally, and importantly

■ What is the contractual notice period on either side? Try to get as much as possible from the employer and as little commitment in respect of yourself. You will probably end up with an equal compromise but there is no harm in trying.

■ What happens if a redundancy situation arises? You should check if there is a severance package in addition to Government statutory minimum terms, and ask what terms will apply to you if the situation arises in your first year of employment.

Remember that a couple of days spent negotiating can win you a salary increase that might otherwise take a couple of years to achieve. Don't be embarrassed in asking for a reasonable salary, no matter how the employer may recoil and posture. Tell yourself that you deserve prosperity and are ready to accept it!

WRITING YOUR ACCEPTANCE LETTER

Once you have decided to accept the job you should confirm it in writing. Remember that your letter willl form part of the 'Contract of Employment', the notional agreement surrounding all aspects of your relationship with the employer. It should therefore contain a number of carefully considered elements along with the pleasantries:

1. Begin your letter with a heading consisting of the job title.

2. Write a short opening paragraph confirming your decision to accept. Suggest that you hope to quickly make a positive contribution. State when you will be starting your new employment.

3. The bullet-point format has got you this far so there is no point in deserting it now.

4. List agreed main terms, each expressed in a short statement:

   ■ salary and agreed review arrangements;

   ■ company car, if applicable;

   ■ benefits such as pension, life assurance, medical, etc.;

   ■ relocation;

   ■ travel expenses;

   ■ other agreed arrangements.

5. The final paragraph can describe your understanding of the agreed responsibilities of the job. Be careful not to promise to achieve the impossible. Conclude with a positive statement that expresses your pleasure in joining the company, relishing the challenge, etc.

An example acceptance letter is given in Figure 17.1.

IN FUTURE, ALWAYS LOOK TO THE FUTURE

Finally, keep your CV in good order and continually review your employment position. You do not have to accept next-best. The PSP system has worked for you once and it will work for you at any future time. You have proven that there are opportunities in the job markets and that you are able to design and implement an effective job-getting campaign.

You can now take command of your own career. There is no reason to remain in an unrewarding or dead-end job ever again.

Good luck for the future!

Figure 17.1 Example acceptance letter

Dear Mr Hollings

IT Officer

Thank you for your letter of 2 February, offering me employment with your organisation. I am pleased to accept the position and greatly look forward to commencing my employment at 9 am on 1 March. My understanding is that I will report to your London office.

As you are aware, we discussed the Terms and Conditions of employment in some detail, and my understanding of our agreement is summarised as follows:

- The initial salary will be £24,000 per annum, and this will be reviewed no later than 1 August 200X.

- The salary is guaranteed and will not be subject to bonus payments.

- I will be eligible to non-contributory health insurance after the first six months of my employment.

- You will provide a company car, based on Band C of the list provided.

- I will receive an interest-free loan to cover the annual cost of a rail season ticket to commute between London and Berkhamsted, to be repayable from salary on a monthly basis.

- The notice period will be three months on either side.

Many thanks for the courtesy shown to me during our discussions. I feel confident in being able to make a positive contribution on your behalf, and look forward to a long association with the Company.

Yours sincerely

Appendix

General competency exercises

These are tough and demanding exercises. The aim is to examine each of the generic competencies to produce suitable examples for your CV and also to enable you to perform well in interviews. These comprise:

- communications skills (see Chapter 2)

- goal orientation

- planning and organising

- problem-solving

- motivating others

- training

- professional standards.

You should do these exercises with some diligence, equipping yourself with a set of model examples that will provide a very strong base for your CV and for your response to interview questions.

The first exercise has already been set out in Chapter 2, and here the second exercise is accompanied by a commentary to illustrate the general method of answering the questions. Subsequently, however, you will get more from the exercises by doing your own analysis, asking yourself why the interviewer is asking each question and what he or she is trying to assess by your answer.

Each exercise concludes with a scoresheet, and the scores will indicate your strengths and also any areas of potential weakness that you need to address.

COMMUNICATIONS
SUMMARY OF EVIDENCE

Assess your own answers in this summary, giving yourself a score from 0 to 6.

			Fails to meet *any part of the* *statement*				*Meets all* *aspects*

Evidence	0 No evidence	1	2	3	4	5	6
Ability to communicate concisely and effectively							
Enjoy talking and dealing with others							
Persuasive skills							
Able to build effective relationships							
Good listening skills							
Able to overcome the resistance of others							
Able to plan and implement effective group communications							

Aggregate score: _____

For each of your past **4** jobs, choose a good example that demonstrates your communication skills (use your previous answers if desired):

1 _____

2 _____

3 _____

4 _____

General competency exercise 2:

Planning and organising

The ability to plan and organise your time, your work programme or a complex project is particularly important. There is a trend to give more responsibility to the individual employee, so good organisational skills are a major and necessary competency.

You must therefore show that you enjoy planning and organising, and can produce plans that are flexible enough to cope with change. In order to do that, you need to consider the process that you would use, and show evidence of it in your CV, job documentation and interview responses.

A typical organisational and planning process essentially involves identifying clear objectives and considering how you might be able to achieve them. That is the main point, but within it are the subsidiary skills of gathering and assessing relevant information, the prioritising of interim goals and the evaluation of available options. You can also show that you meet tight deadlines and work calmly and effectively when under pressure.

Recruiters will want to know if you:

■ make effective forward plans;

■ efficiently marshall available resources;

■ produce realistic schedules;

■ exercise good time management;

■ anticipate and plan for change;

■ produce contingency plans in the event of changing circumstances;

■ handle paperwork and administrative systems in a competent and efficient manner;

■ pay attention to detail.

Guarding against 'deselectors'

Recruiters seek to identify and reject people with undesirable characteristics. The skilled interviewer will probe for potential negatives or areas of suspected weakness. It is important for the applicant to quickly turn the interview to positive factors and concentrate on reasons why the employer should select you – instead of dwelling on analysing why you might not be suitable.

It is certain that an experienced recruiter will be keen to identify and reject shambolic and disorganised people who give little thought to forward planning. The type who cannot analyse problems is of little benefit to employers in this day and age. The type of person who thinks that it will somehow 'come right on the night' will be avoided like the plague. These are obvious cases for rejection. However, the skilled interviewer will also be looking out for the person who makes plans but forgets small, important details, the sort who tries to analyse problems but doesn't quite pull the whole thing off, who makes no contingency plans and is unable to adapt if things change.

YOUR IMAGE

You have clear objectives and know how to prioritise the work needed to achieve them. You enjoy planning and organising, using your ability to identify and take account of all relevant information. You pay attention to detail and can use a rational, logical approach to assess the available options. You recognise potential dangers and anticipate problems, forming contingency plans to cope with changes.

The selectors

The inset panel describes the person you are seeking to portray. If you read the description again and assess how you measure up to the standard you probably come quite close, but you need to demonstrate your ability to the recruiter. Examples of past achievements, preferably resulting in benefits for the employer, are powerful ways of illustrating your ability as an organiser.

Take an A4 pad and work through the following questions, with an emphasis on finding relevant examples from one of your most recent jobs. Try to be reasonably neat in making your notes, and make sure that you retain your answer sheets for future use. This is valuable background work for your CV and interview preparation.

Set 1

(a) Have you ever organised a significant project involving a programme of tasks for yourself or for others? Give an example.

(b) How did you set about the job?

(c) What were the things you had to take account of when planning and organising it?

Demonstrate you are capable of meticulous analysis, setting clear objectives, discussing the issues with colleagues (remember communications), writing down and prioritising tasks, and anticipating problems.

Set 2

(a) When did you have to deal with lots of different kinds of paperwork requiring attention to detail?

(b) Why was it important to pay particular attention to detail?

(c) Do you enjoy work which requires close attention to detail? If so, state the reasons why.

Efficient administration is frequently a part of organisation and planning, even when discussing jobs that, on the face of it, have little or no clerical elements. Company quality assurance systems often involve a very comprehensive records system that relies on great attention to detail and many production workers have to complete various forms on a regular basis.

It is therefore a good idea to demonstrate appropriate ability in this respect.

Set 3

(a) What about contingency planning? Give an example when you had to change your plan to cope with unforeseen circumstances.

(b) What were the main problems that you faced?

(c) How did your original plan cater for this specific possibility?

Change can usually be expected to arise, but often it comes in unexpected forms. You should aim to show an ability to devise plans that that are flexible enough to deal with the most unforeseen event. Note the discrepancy between the first and the third question here: you are asked to state when you had to cope with *unforeseen* circumstances, and then to say how your plan catered for the specific possibility. Quite obviously, if it was a specific possibility, then it was not totally unforeseen. Try to be alert for subtle tricks such as this, and do not be afraid to generally point them out to the interviewer in your reply.

In this case it is recommended that you quote an example where your plan allowed for dangers that you had identified and yet was also generally flexible enough to cope with changes that could not be envisaged.

Set 4

(a) Give an example of a time when you had to plan a project and organise it according to a schedule of interim goals.

(b) What method did you use to plan your schedule?

(c) What problems did you encounter in meeting the deadlines, and how did you deal with them?

Demonstrate a methodical approach with a good grasp of how to devise and implement a timetable. If appropriate, you could choose an example where you used project-planning software to design the schedules, thus also demonstrating your computer-literacy. (A skilful interviewee can achieve two or three objectives with the same answer.)

The problems that you choose to reveal should not be too devastating or it can indicate unrealistic initial planning. On the other hand, there is little that you can do about an unexpected external event – a fire at a suppliers' factory, for example. The main thing is to sshow that your timetable was not too rigid to allow for change.

Set 5

(a) Now give details of a time when you were working under pressure with two or more equally important assignments competing for your time.

(b) What did you do?

(c) How did you decide which things to omit and which things must be done in the time available?

This set of questions is designed to assess your ability to prioritise. Show that you can work calmly and effectively in demanding circumstances, and even thrive on the pressure. (Be careful not to give the impression that this is a regular occurrence, however.) In these circumstances you should describe the compromises that you had to make and show how and why you made any trade-offs. It is important to demonstrate a logical approach, gathering and taking account of available information to make decisions and communicating with others to see which matters can be safely delayed. This also demonstrates teamwork and communication skills.

PLANNING AND ORGANISING
SUMMARY OF EVIDENCE

Assess your own answers in this summary, giving yourself a score from 0 to 6.

Fails to meet
any part of the
statement

Meets all
aspects

Evidence	0 No evidence	1	2	3	4	5	6
Establishes clear objectives							
Enjoys planning and organising							
Formulates effective plans which allow for unforeseen change							
Uses a logical method to identify and evaluate options							
Administrative and clerical skills, with attention to detail							
Effective prioritising skills							
Consistently meets deadlines							

Aggregate score: _____

For each of your past **4** jobs, choose a good example that demonstrates your goal orientation and determination (use your previous answers if desired):

1 _____

2 _____

3 _____

4 _____

GENERAL COMPETENCY EXERCISE 3:

GOAL ORIENTATION

To assess your goal orientation and determination, the interviewer will search for evidence by asking you to give examples of where you have succeeded in the past. You need to demonstrate that you enjoy the opportunity of setting demanding goals for yourself, rather than having targets set for you by others. This gives you something to work for, of course, and you can use strong examples to illustrate that you show determination to achieve your goals. Let the interviewer see that you relish a challenge and persevere to overcome any setbacks.

Deselectors

The interviewer will be alert to any signal that reveals an unambitious applicant who is not target-oriented. The person who prefers undemanding goals set by others is usually easily discouraged by setbacks and rarely achieves high personal standards because he or she does not aim for them.

YOUR IMAGE

You are a proactive person who sets high personal goals. You show drive and determination to achieve targets, and you will still pursue your objectives even when beset by setbacks or changing circumstances. You prefer to set your own challenging goals and use your own initiative to attain them.

Take an A4 pad and answer the following sets of questions. Consider the reasons behind the questions and think carefully about the most suitable responses. Use a separate sheet for each set of questions and answers. Save these answer sheets as a resource for later use.

Set 1

(a) How much experience do you have in working to targets?

(b) Give an example of when you set yourself a demanding target.

(c) How did you set about achieving it and how successful were you?

Set 2

(a) When did you set a goal for yourself?

(b) Why did you choose this goal and what was involved in achieving it?

(c) What setbacks occurred and how did you set about overcoming them?

Set 3

(a) Describe an occasion when you had to show effort and determination over a long period of time to achieve an objective.

(b) How did you maintain your enthusiasm?

(c) How did you set about achieving your objective?

Set 4

(a) Describe a situation where you were faced with a major obstacle or difficulty in achieving a goal.

(b) How did you overcome the problem?

(c) How successful were you in achieving your aims?

Set 5

(a) Describe the most challenging goals or targets in your present/last job.

(b) How have you set about achieving these goals?

(c) How successful have you been and how do you know that?

GOAL ORIENTATION
SUMMARY OF EVIDENCE

Assess your own answers in this summary, giving yourself a score from 0 to 6.

Address any area of weakness by returning to the question and try to produce a more effective answer.

Evidence	0 No evidence	1	2	3	4	5	6
Sets high personal goals							
Effective use of effort and resources to achieve results							
Demonstrates determination to achieve aims							
Displays drive and self-motivation							
Able to overcome the resistance of others							
Can surmount problems and setbacks							
Able to adapt goals if circumstances change							

Aggregate score: _____

For each of your past **4** jobs, choose a good example that demonstrates your goal orientation and determination (use your previous answers if desired):

1 _____

2 _____

3 _____

4 _____

GENERAL COMPETENCY EXERCISE 4:

PERSONAL INTEGRITY

This refers to integrity and confidentiality. Most jobs have their own codes of ethics and it is important to know what they are when making job applications. So, when an interviewer is assessing you as a candidate, he or she wishes to evaluate whether you:

- understand and are able to adhere to any legal and regulatory standards which are required for the position;

- consistently display high standards of personal and professional integrity;

- are committed to achieving high standards;

- can implement company policies;

- can win the confidence of customers/clients on the basis of a high level of integrity and confidentiality.

YOUR IMAGE

You are an honest and upright person who understands the need for high standards and rules. You are flexible in most other aspects of your life but refuse to compromise on standards and integrity. Within this, you can be relied upon to put the customer first, and will always consider the needs of colleagues and of the organisation. You take pains to keep abreast of regulations and legal developments that affect your job.

Set 1

(a) What factors do you take into account when setting standards for your work?

(b) How and why do you choose these factors?

(c) Give an example when circumstances dictated that you reconsider these factors. What did you do?

Set 2

(a) Have you ever felt that your integrity or standards were in danger of being compromised?

(b) How did you respond?

(c) Were you satisfied or dissatisfied with the outcome and why?

Set 3

(a) Describe a time when your own personal standards of integrity were in conflict with those of either a customer, a colleague or the organisation.

(b) What factors did you take into account? How did you proceed and why?

(c) What was the result?

Set 4

(a) Give an example of how you had to comply with accepted standards or laid-down rules and procedures.

(b) What was the particular significance of this?

(c) Give an example when you decided not to follow laid down rules and procedures and say why you made that decision.

PERSONAL INTEGRITY
SUMMARY OF EVIDENCE

Assess your own answers in this summary, giving yourself a score from 0 to 6.

Address any area of weakness by returning to the question and try to produce a more effective answer.

Evidence	0 No evidence	1	2	3	4	5	6
Has high professional standards							
Does not compromise integrity							
Shows an awareness of the values of others							
Understands relevant regulations							
Checks regulations and standards when necessary							
Brings a questioning mind to bear in difficult circumstances							
Sacrifices own needs to those of the company or the customers							

Aggregate score: _____

For each of your past **4** jobs, choose a good example that demonstrates your professional integrity (use your previous answers if desired):

1 _____

2 _____

3 _____

4 _____

General competency exercise 5:

Problem-solving

This general competency concerns a very underrated core skill. You will score highly by ensuring that your CV demonstrates strong ability as a problem-solver.

Recruiters are always seeking problem-solvers. All companies and organisations are blighted with problems. Most problems are not new – they are either lurking in the background and waiting to happen, or they have already happened and are 'on the back-burner' awaiting a solution.

When responding to questions at an interview, remember that for every problem there are two main approaches:

1. You can do something about the problem immediately – some situations are just too threatening and dangerous for procrastination.

2. You can recognise and assess the problem and then decide to wait. This is often a valid approach if correctly applied. You make the most of the relative calm but anticipate the day when the monster will suddenly leap at your throat with fangs bared.

Which line you take in any specific instance will depend on the circumstances. In the latter case, however, you must have a contingency plan. Prospective employers want to see that you can cope with their problems and deal with them effectively.

Interviewers will try to discover if you:

- are able to quickly and accurately recognise potential *relevant* problems;

- can identify and gather relevant information;

- can relate and cross-check different kinds information from varying sources;

- are able to use the information in a logical manner;

- can make the correct decision;

- are prepared to use different and novel solutions when necessary.

YOUR IMAGE

You *enjoy* problem-solving and are always vigilant for potential risks. When you identify early warning signs, you use a systematic approach and a wide range of analytical skills to assess the full situation. You first ensure that it is a relevant problem, you check facts, ask questions and compare information from different sources. You are aware of your own strengths but you are also prepared to ask for help from people with specialist knowledge.

Most importantly, you use good judgement, based on all known facts, to reach an effective decision. And you are not afraid to use an unconventional solution when the situation demands it. However, you are also 'a safe pair of hands', and will not do anything outrageous and against company policies.

The conscientious interviewer will reject the candidate who:

- obviously dislikes problem-solving and avoids even looking for warning signs;

- is afraid of problems and would not would not dare to attempt an innovative solution.

Neither would the manager be keen on the applicant who:

- either does not know how to identify and gather the necessary information or who does not know how to use available data;

- does not systematically assess the situation and therefore often fails to addresses the real issues;

- will sometimes recklessly ignore looming dangers.

Set 1

(a) In your present/last job, what kind of problems did the employer face and how did you you set about solving them?

(b) On the evidence of your most recent/previous job, describe your main strengths in analysing and solving problems.

(c) Which sort of problems did you most enjoy dealing with?

Set 2

Give details of a situation when you had to collect facts to inform a decision or solve a problem.

(a) How did you set about collecting the information?

(b) What steps did you take to make sure that the information you gathered was correct and relevant?

(c) How did you use it in making your decision?

Set 3

(a) Give an example of when a particular problem was identified in a personal work setting

(b) Who identified the problem and how was it identified?

(c) Having recognised the problem, what steps did you take to resolve it?

Set 4

(a) Describe a situation where you designed and implemented a novel and creative solution to a particular problem.

(b) Why did you feel that a different kind of approach was needed?

(c) What other options did you consider?

Set 5

(a) Produce an example of when you identified a potential problem and had to alert a more senior person.

(b) How did you collect and organise the information to assist you in making a decision?

(c) How did you present your solution for approval by the senior person?

PROBLEM-SOLVING
SUMMARY OF EVIDENCE

Assess your own answers in this summary, giving yourself a score from 1 to 6.

Address any area of weakness by returning to the question and try to produce a more effective answer.

EVIDENCE	0 No evidence	1	2	3	4	5	6
Able to quickly recognise potential problems							
Able to identify and gather relevant information							
Gathers data from different sources and cross-checks to validate							
Able to use information in a logical manner							
Able to make the right decisions							
Able to surmount problems and setbacks							
Prepared to use novel and innovative solutions							

Aggregate score: _____

For each of your past **4** jobs, choose a good example that demonstrates your ability to solve problems (use your previous answers if desired):

1 _____

2 _____

3 _____

4 _____

GENERAL COMPETENCY EXERCISE 6:

TEAMWORK AND MOTIVATING OTHERS

Teamworking is one of the key modern concepts in industry and commerce. Recruiters still try to find the most impressive individual for the job but, increasingly, they are particularly looking for the appropriate person for each place within a team. This approach recognises that too many natural leaders in the same team can cause friction. The well-focused job-getter therefore has to be aware of the kind of role that is available and tailor the image accordingly.

That said, natural leaders need to lead, and natural followers are unhappy when leadership is thrust upon them. Any applicant who consciously aims for an unsuitable job should have a good personal reason because it is a sure way of accruing future work problems.

YOUR IMAGE

You are a proactive team member who enjoys working in open and collaborative teams. You readily adapt to new people and work environments, and demonstrate an understanding of how to blend your skills with those possessed by other people. Also, you are a person who sets a good example, with a good comprehension of how to motivate and encourage others.

However, whether as a team leader or team member, any candidate should give evidence that they are proactive and can motivate other people.

Your presentation should provide the following evidence:

- your ability to encourage the efforts of other people, providing them with support and valuing their contributions;

- emphasising the objectives and targets of the team, creating enthusiasm for the achievement of goals;

- that you use relevant and appropriate ways to motivate others, creating good working relations and maintaining a pleasant work environment;

- an understanding of the needs of others;

- enthusiasm in sharing and jointly developing ideas.

Demonstrate how you adapt to the characteristics, desires and needs of different people, and how you overcome difficulties.

Motivating individuals

You should aim to provide evidence that you have a good understanding of how to motivate on a one-to-one basis. This includes recognising and understanding the needs of the other person. It is important to show that you test the relevance and success of your efforts. Your answers should demonstrate that you give encouragement and feedback on how well the others are doing.

Motivating groups

Recognise that motivating a group presents different issues and problems from those encountered in motivating an individual. For example, team members may have conflicting personal interests and ambitions.

> Building effective teams is more important in some situations than in others. Look for signs of rapid change as this usually indicates a need for cohesive teamwork. This also applies when there is great competition and when quick, effective decisions are required. In these circumstances, the employer will want to build a team of differing skills and attributes. Try to establish what type of skills the recruiter is seeking by telephoning for an informal discussion about the job.

Different people have differing motivational styles. However, even as a team leader, you should demonstrate that you *motivate* the group rather than *direct* it. Other key points are that you:

- motivate the group members to share ideas and work as a team;

- have an insight into the aspirations of team members, and take account of them;

- monitor the situation and take early steps to address problems;

- treat the other team members both as colleagues and as internal customers.

You must show that you positively relish the opportunity to work in a team. Moreover, you believe that the success of the overall team equates to your own personal success and that all individual team members have a vital contribution to make.

Your CV and interview answers should reflect that you use your initiative to be a useful team member and help the group as a whole. Within this, you work efficiently and accurately, meeting personal deadlines and contribute to the achievement of the team's overall time and quality targets.

Set 1

(a) Give an example of when you had to work within a team.

(b) What did you perceive your contribution to be and how successful were you?

(c) What do you enjoy about working in a team?

Set 2

(a) Describe a situation where you were the member/leader of a team that achieved a demanding goal.

(b) What was your personal contribution to the team's success?

(c) How did you motivate and encourage other team members?

Set 3

(a) Describe a situation where it was necessary to motivate an individual.

(b) How did the other person react?

(c) How did you test whether your efforts were successful and what feedback did you give to the other person?

Set 4

(a) When have you had to persuade a person or a group to take part in something against their initial wishes?

(b) How did you overcome their resistance and motivate them to participate?

(c) When they took part in the activity, what feedback did you give to the other people?

SET 5

(a) Describe a situation when you had to lead by example.

(b) What steps did you take?

(c) How did you gauge your success?

TEAMWORK
SUMMARY OF EVIDENCE

Assess your own answers in this summary, giving yourself a score from 1 to 6.

Evidence	0 No evidence	1	2	3	4	5	6
Understands how to motivate others							
Leads by example							
Shows good insight into team situations							
Adapts to change and other's needs							
Promotes a good teamworking environment							
Motivates rather than leads							
Can overcome problems and setbacks							

Aggregate score: _____

For each of your past **4** jobs, choose a good example that demonstrates your teamworking and motivational ability (use your previous answers if desired):

1 _____

2 _____

3 _____

4 _____

Recommended job search bibliography

Be Prepared! Getting Ready for Job Interviews, Julie-Ann Amos, How To Books

Handling Tough Job Interviews, Julie-Anne Amos, How to Books

How to Master Psychometric Tests, Mark Parkinson, Kogan Page

Occupations, DfES Publications

Passing Psychometric Tests, Andrea Shavick, How To Books

Returning to Work, Sally Longson, How To Books

Starting Your Own Business, Jim Green, How to Books

Sweaty Palms – The Neglected Art of Being Interviewed, H. Anthony Medley, Ten Speed Press

The Career Change Handbook, Graham Green, How To Books

The Perfect CV, Max Eggert, Random House

The Perfect Interview, Max Eggert, Random House

The Ultimate CV for Managers and Professionals, Rachel Bishop-Firth, How to Books

What Colour is Your Parachute?, Richard Nelson Bolles, Ten Speed Press

Write a Great CV, Paul McGee, How To Books

Index